MALE SUPREMACY 101

When Women Are Forced to Choose Marriage or Faith

Umm Zakiyyah

Male Supremacy 101: When Women Are Forced to Choose Marriage or Faith
by Umm Zakiyyah

Paperback ISBN: 978-1-942985-23-5
KDP Hardcover ISBN: 979-8-275204-20-9

Library of Congress Control Number: 2025925660

- Join Feminine Soul Reset (FSR) at **SQsoul.com**
- UZ Books at **uzauthor.com**
- UZ Courses at **uzhearthub.com**

Arabic script of Qur'an from legacy.quran.com

Translation of meanings of verses from Qur'an adapted from Saheeh International, Darussalam, and Yusuf Ali translations.

Published by Al-Walaa Publications
Dallas, Texas (USA)

TABLE OF CONTENTS

AUTHOR'S NOTE

This is my Brené Brown book, that's what I'm calling it. And what I mean by that is this. Some years ago, the famous, bestselling author Brené Brown did a TedTalk that went viral. She spoke from her heart about her own vulnerabilities in life and how she ultimately came to see them as her strength, and how other people should see their struggles similarly. This talk spearheaded Brené's career as a guru on transforming your weaknesses into strengths.

But that's not why I'm calling this my Brené Brown book. I'm not aiming for this book to go viral or for it to spearhead any career as a guru of any sort. I'm calling this my Brené Brown book because of something she said in an interview years after that famous TedTalk.

At some point in the interview, the interviewer asked her something to the effect of, "When you look at that talk today, how do you feel?" And she said something I never expected: "I never watched it." The interviewer was surprised, as was I. "Never?" they asked. "Never," she said. "But why?" they asked. "Because I can't bring myself to." Then she explained that she'd poured her heart out in that talk, and she decided to just leave it at that.

This is the book you're holding, me pouring my heart out without filter. It's also the first book I've ever written that I didn't read cover to cover after I finished. It's the first book I've written that I didn't either edit myself or hire someone to do it on my behalf. I didn't want anyone to say anything to make me doubt myself or lose my strength, not because of any typos or grammatical mistakes. But because of the raw truth I was saying behind my imperfect words, even with all my inevitable human mistakes. So, this book you hold, this is my organized chaos—the organized chaos of my heart.

I'm just going to let this book be whatever it is, typos and emotionalism and all.

But keep in mind, I *am* a recovering perfectionist, so I tried my best to get everything right the first time around, formatting and all. And I'm hoping I did a pretty good job.

Also, so much of what I've put in this book—along with my vulnerable, bleeding heart—was borrowed from things I'd already written over the years, including some previously published blogs, some heartfelt journal reflections, and some unpublished manuscripts. So, it's not a "rough draft" in the technical sense of the word.

But some parts of it were certainly rough to draft.

I even cried like a baby in some parts.

I say all that to say, for me, this book encapsulates that famous saying we often hear: *It is what it is.*

So, please forgive me for any emotional triggers it brings up, any insensitive language, or just plain oversights. Beneath it all, I hope you hear my heart, a heart full of love and hope.

And I hope it inspires this ummah, especially our men, to do a better job showing up for us, especially in the name of Islam.

Sincerely,
Your sister in faith and hope,

Umm Zakiyyah
October 27, 2025
5th of Jumada I 1447 AH

اَتَّخَذُوٓاْ أَحْبَارَهُمْ وَرُهْبَٰنَهُمْ أَرْبَابًا مِّن دُونِ ٱللَّهِ وَٱلْمَسِيحَ ٱبْنَ مَرْيَمَ وَمَآ أُمِرُوٓاْ إِلَّا لِيَعْبُدُوٓاْ إِلَٰهًا وَٰحِدًا ۖ لَّآ إِلَٰهَ إِلَّا هُوَ ۚ سُبْحَٰنَهُۥ عَمَّا يُشْرِكُونَ ۝

"They have taken their scholars [or rabbis and priests] and monks as lords besides Allah, and [also] the Messiah, the son of Mary. And they were not commanded except to worship one God; there is no deity except Him. Exalted is He above whatever they associate with Him."

—Qur'an (*At-Tawbah*, The Repentance) 9:31

7

INTRODUCTION
Male Supremacy vs. Divine Supremacy
At a Glance

Male Supremacy Western Model of Religion	Divine Supremacy Islamic Model of Religion
man-centered: i.e., pleasing men is at the center of the human soul	soul-centered: i.e., pleasing Allah is at the center of the human soul
Life Purpose = serving and pleasing a man	Life Purpose = serving and pleasing Allah
Men take priority over Allah: Husband comes first then Allah, so serving and pleasing a man is the path to pleasing Allah. So a woman's husband acts as an "intermediary" between her and Allah, as she has no access to Allah without him.	Allah takes priority over men (and all creation): Allah comes first then your husband, so serving and pleasing Allah is the path to serving or pleasing any of His creation (parents, spouse, etc.)
Manhood is lived outside-in (performative masculinity) He needs external validation to feel like a man, so he seeks proof of his manhood through how far others (esp. women) sacrifice, shrink, and self-erase for him. Performs for the male gaze in hyper-masculinity, seeking cool points from other men.	Manhood is lived inside-out (taqwaa-centered manhood) Manhood is cultivated from inner work, soul-care, and fulfilling his responsibilities regardless of how others show up, even his own wife and children (e.g. Prophets Noah and Lot). Does good deeds for Allah, seeking divine blessings and reward.
Male leadership is a "superior birthright"	Manhood is a weighty, divinely-assigned trust and responsibility
A woman's value in life is based on how desirable she is to a man and/or how well she is serving a man.	A woman's value in life is based on how pleasing she is to Allah and how well she is serving Him.

Every breath a woman takes lowers her worth (i.e., ageing = low value)	Every breath she takes increases her worth, as she's earning more good deeds. Deen and good character = high value
Hate feminism more than they love Islam = rejecting (or trivializing) parts of Islam that look similar to feminism (e.g., women's rights in Islam, honoring women, showing compassion to women, etc.)	Love of Allah and Islam over everything = accepting ALL goodness and truth, even if it overlaps beliefs systems contrary to Islam or worldly movements that have iterations that aren't Islamic
Fear feminism more than they fear Allah = indulge in sin, evil, or dhulm (i.e., disobeying Islam) to harm or slander women in effort to fight against any evidence of women's "independence" or living a life that doesn't center a man	Taqwaa and fear of Allah guides their behavior even when ego is hurt or they feel angry (e.g., the Prophet ﷺ remained a safe person even when stressed due to his wives' behavior, and just took time to self vs. harming them)
Women are ego-boosters and conduits of masculinity	Women are partners and soul companions
The goal is subjugation, control, and mistreatment	The goal is protection, loving connection, and good treatment
Providers of trauma (for women), and protectors of their egos and themselves.*	Providers of provision for women, and protectors of women's wellbeing and safety.
Mercy and *husnu dhann* (best assumption) to men and their faults; extra level of cruelty, unkindness, and *soo'u dhann* (worst assumption) to women and faults/choices.	Mercy and *husnu dhann* (best assumption) to all believers (men and women); extra level of kindness, compassion, and gentleness to women, regardless of faults/choices.

*adapted from the description of modern-day patriarchy (vs. historical patriarchy) given by the lawyer Lena Nguyen.

Prologue
What If Marriage Takes Away Half Her Deen?

I had no idea this would become a book. I thought the things I discuss here would be written under a different title and for a different reason. And that "different reason?" I'm not even sure I have the words just yet. But I do know the reason for *this* book should have been the reason all along: to give that hurting and healing little girl inside me something she could hold in her hands. Something that says to her, *I get it. I hear you. I believe you. And what's happening to you is not okay.*

I'm hoping that this is what this book says to other hurting and healing little girls reading it, even if they're now grown women.

And for the hurting and healing little boys inside the bodies of grown men? I'll let them decide what this book says to them…

Where Do I Even Begin?

In a way, I guess I started writing this book years ago. I just didn't know it at the time. So then, I suppose it's safe to say,

I started and stopped this book over and over again before I even knew it would become this book.

In the beginning, I put together heartfelt reflections and chapters of books by different titles and with text reworded a million times over. I tried to say it all in a way that didn't hurt so much. And still, on the re-read, I'd scared myself half to death. It seemed that no way I put the words together wouldn't equal hurt, for me or someone else.

And I didn't like that.

So, I couldn't bring myself to say all these things out loud, at least not in black-and-white words on a page. It was *too* honest and *too* scary. And I simply wasn't strong enough for that, no matter what other people thought.

Then I decided to take parts of what I'd written and put them in new books with different titles with lighter topics. Yet still, when I got to the parts about women's suffering in the name of religion, there was no way to make that not hurt. So, I gave up. Or maybe I should say I gave in.

Either way, the book you hold in your hand is more than just one book. That's the only way I felt able to put my words together. So, parts of this book are from books I haven't even published yet (and maybe never will), most notably, *What If Marriage Takes Away Half Her Deen?*

Other parts of this book are extracted and adapted from my UZ Newsletter blog that I share with my email list. But even then, I've added a bit more reflection for clarification and context.

I'm calling this book *Male Supremacy 101* because what I've written is really just scratching the surface. It's just a brief introduction to the topic, sort of like if you were enrolling in an intro-level course about it in school. It might seem like it's more than just scratching the surface, but it's not. There really is so much more that could (and should) be said about male supremacy in Muslim spaces.

Oh yeah, I should have mentioned that before. In this book, I'm focusing mainly on how this shows up in the context of Islamic spirituality, though I know it shows up in nearly all religions (and non-religions) today. It is what it is.

"Why don't you just call it patriarchy?" some people might ask. In fact, some people have pretty much asked exactly this, especially when I've spoken about this topic online.

So, to put it simply, I don't call it patriarchy because I think the term *male supremacy* is more accurate and to the point.

Patriarchy historically has other meanings besides male supremacy, as it's often thought of as merely the male version of matriarchy, and in my view, male supremacy is much more problematic than that.

At the same time, I do recognize that for many people, most people, in fact, the word patriarchy is more accurate and to the point. And that's fine. So, if you prefer the word *patriarchy*, then go with that. As with all things, the label matters less than the truth beneath it. And that's what I hope to uncover in this book.

Thank you for reading, by the way.

I appreciate you, I'm grateful for you, and I'm so glad you're here.

"Verily, you (Muslims) will follow the path of those before you, step by step and inch by inch; [such that] if they entered the hole of a lizard, you would follow." We (the Companions) said, "O Messenger of Allah, do you mean the Jews and Christians?" The Prophet ﷺ said, "Who else?"

—Prophet Muhammad, peace be upon him
(Sahih Bukhari 3269, Sahih Muslim 2669)

PART ONE

Who Owns Her Soul?
Choosing Marriage *or* Deen

"The fact that we are continually treated as if we cannot be trusted with our own spiritual autonomy is really at the crux of why so many [Muslim] women are having faith crisis."

—Layla Graham, Qur'an teacher, *haafidhah*, and founder of Prime Learning Resources

One

Who Owns a Woman's Soul?

"**I**f a woman is allowed to follow whatever scholars and *fiqh* opinions she believes are right," the imam said, "then the man has no real role or purpose in the marriage." (In Islam the term *fiqh* generally refers to permissible scholarly opinions on various religious topics).

I burst into laughter. I didn't mean to react this way, and I certainly didn't intend to be rude. But this was my genuine, gut reaction: *He's got to be kidding.* And for a split second, I honestly thought the imam *was* joking. I mean, here was a remarkably intelligent, well-respected member of the Muslim community, and we were in this Zoom meeting precisely for the purpose of planning events to inform women of their Islamic rights in marriage. So, my initial thought was, *He can't possibly believe what he's saying.*

In my defense, there *were* moments in our previous meetings that the imam (who was also a therapist) had indeed been joking. Like myself, it was part of his personality to use sarcastic humor to make a point. So, if we were discussing, for example, advising women to think up questions to ask a potential spouse, the imam might say something like, "Let's wait on that one because we'll need a fatwa to make sure it's permissible for a woman to *think* at all."

So, I imagined that his statement about a man having no meaningful role or purpose in marriage if a woman had the final say in her own religious practice and understanding of her faith was made in the same humorous spirit.

Unfortunately, I was wrong.

The imam's expression conveyed a trace of annoyance and offense in response to my laughter. Then he said, "The entire purpose of Allah assigning the man as the *qawwaam* (leader and protector of women) is to be in charge of things like this."

I creased my forehead in confusion. "And what if the woman has more Islamic knowledge than the man?" I asked.

"Women should only marry men who have more knowledge than they do," he said.

My jaw dropped—almost. In truth, I did everything I could to keep my expression composed. "That's a really dangerous perspective," I said, choosing my words carefully. "It's assumptions like these that make men feel justified in spiritually abusing women."

He didn't openly disagree with this, but he also didn't budge from his original point.

"Some of my friends and clients are healing from emotional trauma they suffered because their husband had that mindset," I continued. "Their husband wanted to prevent them from learning more than he did. So, he'd block his wife from going to certain classes."

I added, "And I know of at least two separate cases where the husband physically assaulted his wife whenever he saw her memorizing the Qur'an. He'd physically attack her because the mere sight of her studying the Qur'an triggered in him a fear that she'd become 'superior' to him in religious knowledge."

"Well, men shouldn't do that," the imam said, his tone sincere and subdued. "The Sunnah obligates men to treat women kindly."

While they prevent their wives from knowing more than they do? I asked in my head. But I kept that sarcastic quip to myself. Instead, I decided to take a different approach given the imam's own background in Islamic studies: "If the entire role of the man being assigned as the *qawwaam* in marriage is to have the final say in which scholars and religious opinions a woman follows, then why does Allah allow a Muslim man to marry a Jewish or Christian woman?"

The imam was quiet.

"Isn't he her *qawwaam* too?" I asked. "Yet in Islam, it's forbidden for a man to force his Jewish or Christian wife to become Muslim. He's not even allowed to prevent her from worshipping God as she chooses, even though Islam views her religious practice as incorrect."

I added, "If that's the freedom of choice that Allah obligates a man to honor when his wife doesn't even believe in Him properly, how is it possible that someone who fully submits to Him and accepts Islam has *less* rights to her soul?"

The imam said nothing to that, but I could tell he was becoming irritated with me. So, rather than respond to my question, he changed the subject entirely.

In the end, he accused me of being influenced by my own unhealed trauma in thinking women should be allowed to have the final say in what they genuinely felt was most correct for their souls and religious practice. While I fully own that my trauma definitely influenced my perspective (and still does), I also realize that this isn't necessarily a *bad* thing.

Sometimes it takes a traumatic experience (or a series of life-changing events) to return us to our fitrah, and thus inspire us to realign our mindsets and lives with how we should have been thinking and living all along. For example, if a die-hard atheist goes through the traumatic experience of being caught in a storm out in the middle of the sea, similar to the scenario discussed in the Qur'an, is it a *bad thing* if this experience leaves him so shaken that he never lets go of the spiritual health of his soul ever again?

While this analogy might be difficult for an outsider looking in to understand, it is quite apt as it relates to my own emotional and spiritual experience within my nafs and treatment of "men in authority" in my life. I was getting dangerously close to prioritizing the authority of men over the authority of Allah. In the inner world of my own nafs, that type of (at best) subtle shirk is what *not* having this clause in my marriage contract would mean for me (though I understand this won't necessarily be the case for all women). So, yes, my trauma did in fact create a storm at the sea of my emotions and I fear I would drown without having a guarantee that I have the right to hold on to the rope of my Rabb directly, without having to use my husband as a spiritual "intermediary."

In the end, with regards to the imam, it was clear he didn't see his own trauma clearly; he only saw mine. Ultimately, it became obvious to me that he was projecting his own unacknowledged trauma onto me (and unacknowledged trauma is exponentially worse than trauma that is merely not fully healed, because you can't heal what you don't acknowledge exists in the first place). It was quite obvious that he was so deeply influenced by his own unacknowledged emotional wounds that he had both internalized and Islamicized them—until the wounded masculine that lived within his nafs became not only the core of his spiritual practice, but also the core of his identity itself.

And this terrified me, not only for his sake, but also for the sake of the entire ummah.

After all, this was a well-respected imam. This imam himself was often invited to speak at Islamic conferences and events throughout the United States (and beyond). He additionally facilitated numerous Muslim marriage programs in a variety of communities. In fact, part of what he was most well-known for was the compassionate support he offered women who were healing from emotional or spiritual trauma they'd sustained in marriage. That was how I myself learned of him, through the referral of those who had sought his counseling or directly benefited from his work.

Yet even *he* didn't believe a woman's soul was her own.

This was one of those chilling moments that I saw up-close and personal the terrifying real-time manifestation—and spiritually damaging implications—of what was discussed in this famous prophetic hadith about the Signs of the Last Day:

> "Allah does not take away the knowledge, by taking it away from (the hearts of) the people, but takes it away by the death of the religious learned men till when none of the (religious learned men) remains, people will take as their leaders ignorant persons who when consulted will give their verdict without knowledge. So, they will go astray and will lead the people astray" (Bukhari: Book 1: Volume 3: Hadith 100).

Two

Forced to Choose Marriage or Deen

Y*ou can be Muslim or you can be married.* This is the sinking realization that settled on me as I considered the personal implications of acquiescing to the imam's perspective on the husband's "right" to the final say in a woman's understanding of religious matters that directly affected the health of her soul. *But you can't be both.*

As I write this, it has been some time since that fateful Zoom meeting with the imam, but it's a conversation that I doubt I'll ever forget.

Each time I reflect on the imam's words, they highlight for me another layer of the dark side of so much that's happening beneath the surface in our spiritual communities. It also makes me understand in a deeply intimate way the profound Qur'anic lesson that highlights how it is often those who think they're doing the most good in the world that are foremost in causing the most destruction, corruption, and harm:

وَإِذَا قِيلَ لَهُمْ لَا تُفْسِدُوا۟ فِى ٱلْأَرْضِ قَالُوٓا۟ إِنَّمَا نَحْنُ مُصْلِحُونَ ۝

21

أَلَا إِنَّهُمْ هُمُ ٱلْمُفْسِدُونَ وَلَٰكِن لَّا يَشْعُرُونَ ﴿١٢﴾

**"And when it is said to them, 'Do not cause corruption
on the earth,' they say, 'We are only those setting
things aright.' Verily, they are the ones causing
corruption, but they perceive not.'"**
—*Al-Baqarah*, 2:11-12

This experience with the well-respected imam also gives
me a deeper understanding of why so many Muslim women
are suffering so deeply and pervasively, and why so many of
their wounds are ultimately irreparable during their spiritual
sojourn in this world.

These women are having nervous breakdowns, are
battling depression, and are drowning in spiritual crisis that
they see no way out of. And because of views like the
imam's—which define Islam itself as a religious way of life
that *forces* women to emotionally *and* spiritually abandon
themselves and that *requires* men to dominate women's lives
and souls (even if the man has a weak or flimsy spiritual
foundation himself)—women are collapsing internally.
Consequently, there no longer remains within the woman's
emotionally exhausted and spiritually wounded *nafs*—that
complex inner world of the mind, heart, and nervous system
that defines the essence of the self—any more room for
"Islam" itself.

The Deeper Darkness of Spiritual Crisis in Women

Given this somber spiritual reality, it should come as no
surprise that many Muslim women are leaving Islam entirely.
The exact amount or numerical percentage of these women
is far too hidden (and numerous) to accurately count,
officially or unofficially.

The utter impossibility of calculating an even *relatively* accurate percentage of these spiritually checked-out women is due to very phenomenon that sent them into spiritual crisis in the first place: It is neither emotionally nor spiritually safe—and it is often, in fact, socially and personally *dangerous*—for a Muslim woman to show up in any way that suggests, let alone outright claims, that she has a right to her own life and soul.

If this is the case for a Muslim woman merely following a fiqh opinion that a man doesn't like or agree with, how much more so if a woman openly admits that she has internally checked-out of believing in Islam at all? For this reason, the vast majority of Muslim women whose spiritual crisis reaches this destructive level are far more inclined (socially and religiously) toward "quiet quitting" Islam than openly quitting it.

This is especially the case for the large number of Muslim women who are for all intents and purposes fully trapped in their toxic, dysfunctional, or abusive marriages.

These are women who had, in a sincere effort toward being a good Muslim woman or a righteous wife, equated female helplessness with Islamic piety and "femininity." As a result of having internalized this ideology of false piety rooted in appeasing the wounded masculine, many of these women have absolutely no practical or financial resources of their own.

In the beginning of their marriages, these women had genuinely believed it was their Islamic obligation—or at least what was most pleasing to Allah—to give up literally everything of this world and focus solely on centering their entire lives around their husband and children. Consequently, they end up years later with absolutely no financial literacy, no marketable skills, and nothing tangibly valuable of their own should they desire or choose another life for themselves.

Not coincidentally, this end result for women in spiritual crisis or in emotional turmoil in their marriages is precisely the *goal* of in circles of false piety rooted in the collective wounded masculine, which presents itself as the sole torchbearers of authentic Islamic practice. This goal is also why women who speak out against this are swiftly labeled "feminist" (or "bitter" if they are divorced or unmarried while giving cautionary advice to other women). It is also precisely why circles of false piety genuinely fear feminism more than they fear Allah.

When a woman who previously ascribed to this spiritually destructive ideology of false piety (which she mistook for Islam itself) finds herself forced to choose between her marriage and her deen, she often chooses her marriage. This is because staying married is quite literally the most practical option for her—even if it is also the most obviously spiritually harmful in her particular case.

Then this hurting female soul quietly lives a life of ever-deepening inner darkness as she goes through the motions of being a dutiful Muslim wife. Yet deep inside she has already "checked out" of Islam, which in her experience is a religious way of life that requires women to suffer continuously in this world, even requiring a woman to abandon the spiritual needs of her own soul, if this is what makes her husband feel like a *qawwaam* in his household.

Three

Not All Women

Before I continue, I think it's essential to clarify, and in fact emphasize, an important point: I realize that not *all* women would care about this type of stipulation in the contract. Additionally, I fully understand that from both a personal and Islamic perspective, this clause isn't in itself a *necessity* in every Muslim woman's marriage agreement.

At the same time, in all honesty, it is my genuine belief that for any Muslim woman of today to neglect this clause is to unnecessarily subject herself to the risk of long-term emotional and spiritual harm, even if this harm is emanates primarily from her own inner world of the nafs. This long-term harm is especially more imminent if she is not living in a culture or circumstance wherein she is protected by both sincere Muslim male relatives *and* by a righteous Muslim government who upholds the Sunnah of honoring women and respecting their rights to boundaries and human choice.

As such, I myself strongly caution any woman against leaving off putting this spiritual boundary in writing, even if she sincerely imagines she wouldn't need it because, for example, she is marrying a "good man" or because what is being conveyed is "extraneous" and "unnecessary." While I agree that, spiritually speaking, this clause is technically extraneous since it states in a marriage contract what has already been established by our Creator in the Qur'an—i.e. the sole responsibility of every human being, male and female, to protect his or her own soul from harm, even if someone with authority over them wishes to compel them (intentionally or unintentionally) toward spiritual self-harm—my strong caution is due to six (6) main reasons:

1) If you are truly marrying a good man and thus really don't "need" this clause, then he would have absolutely no problem signing it. This is because respecting this spiritual boundary would come naturally to him if he is genuinely good man. Moreover, a truly good man would be *naturally* motivated to do everything within his power and capability to make you feel emotionally and spiritually safe before he asks or expects you to fully trust him as a husband and leader in the home—let alone before he expects you to assign to him all the privileges of being a "good man."

2) Requiring this clause in the contract can (and should) act as a "red flag alert" toward any man who either refuses to sign it or who goes back on his word after he does.

3) Even if you yourself believe, as a general rule, that you should follow your husband's fiqh opinion in nearly everything, in a healthy relationship, this should come from the sincerity and conviction of your own heart, as sincerity and conviction are the essence of spiritual wellness of the soul, which is, after all, the goal of any religious practice. In reaching this point of sincerity and conviction, there should be, for example, respectful discussions between you and your husband, not the perpetual assumption that any and every opinion your

26

husband has is automatically best and healthiest for *your* soul.

4) In order for a man to genuinely believe you are *obligated* to follow his fiqh opinion in everything, and in order for a man to genuinely believe that it is he, not you yourself, who has the final say in matters pertaining to the health and wellness of *your* soul, he must first, even if only unconsciously, see your role as a servant of Allah as *inferior* to your role as a wife to him. However, in Islam, the exact opposite is true.

5) Due to the vulnerable role that a woman has been assigned in marriage, especially to a man she is only beginning to get to know intimately, it is almost always better to chance putting *more* protections than necessary in place, rather than less. As the saying goes, "Better safe than sorry." And any man who sincerely cares about you and your spiritual well-being and who is genuinely invested in keeping you safe from harm would fully agree.

6) In these Last Days, there are ever-increasing cases of women having mental breakdowns, women facing spiritual crises, and women even leaving Islam entirely as a result of the gradual, almost imperceptible wearing down of her spirit, which very often occurs in marriage. These are typically cases wherein the woman sought to submit to her husband so completely that there were effectively no boundaries (emotionally, physically, or spiritually) between her and her husband. And nearly every single of these women began their marriage convinced they were marrying a "good man." More significantly, many of these women were in fact married to a "good man" who, in the end, made choices that harmed her emotional and spiritual world, even though in the beginning, he didn't consciously intend to cause

27

her harm. In these cases, this clause in the marriage contract could have protected them *both* from regret.

Also, I would gently challenge my sisters in faith to sit with themselves and honestly ask themselves this question: *If a man genuinely believes I cannot and should not be trusted with the most basic task of every human in this world—taking care of my own soul—why is he marrying me at all?*

Four

Pitfalls of Naiveté, Innocence, and Inexperience

In all honesty, until I met the imam, in my more than twenty-five years of studying Qur'an and fiqh and reading dozens of fatwas and books by scholars (past and present) and traveling the world, I had never heard a single person—scholar or layperson, male or female—equate the entire *definition* and purpose of qawwaamah with a man deciding what fiqh views a woman follows. However, over the years, I have spoken to women who held a religious point of view that would essentially agree with him.

These are women who wholeheartedly agree with almost *any* religious perspective that severely restricts a woman's rights to her own mind and soul, so long as some man somewhere at some time (historically or presently) has attached this anti-woman perspective to "the Qur'an and Sunnah." They believe that the only line that a woman has the right to draw in marriage is when she is being asked to neglect a clear religious obligation or when she is being asked to indulge in a clear prohibition. Otherwise, she effectively has no rights to draw a single boundary with her own body, mind, and soul.

Once upon a time, I myself was this woman.

So, I know firsthand the unspeakable harm this type of religious misogyny afflicts on every single part of the woman's nafs—body, mind, and soul—usually after years and years of genuinely thinking she was living the life of a "good Muslim woman."

Over the years, I have spoken to women who have had no experiential understanding of what this type of long-term spiritual harm to the nafs even means. As a result, in the eyes of these women, the possibility that she *herself* could (or would) sustain deep spiritual wounds as a result of neglecting a simple clausal protection of her soul in her marriage contract is inconceivable, especially when she is first embarking on marriage.

We All Start Off Sincere, Inexperienced, and Naïve

At the start of our marriage journey, the vast majority of women (myself included) tend to naively believe, as mentioned to in the previous chapter: *If you're marrying a good man, you wouldn't need that type of stipulation in a marriage contract.* So, they'll say things like, "If you feel the need to put that in a marriage contract, you shouldn't be getting married!" or "If you need to put something like that in writing, then you're not marrying a good man!"

Undoubtedly, these naïve points of view quite obviously contradict the Qur'anic instructions and prophetic guidance related to how believers should handle contracts involving future obligations. At the same time, in Islam it is not technically *haraam* (religiously forbidden) for a Muslim to avoid having a written contract of personal protection in these cases. Yes, it is certainly the case that these divine guidelines were given to the best "good Muslims" of all time (i.e. the prophetic Companions) and *they* certainly didn't believe that their high status as "good Muslims" protected them from the need to put clausal protections in place.

Nevertheless, in Islam, no matter what our status is or is not in front of Allah, it remains each person's prerogative and personal choice what they choose (or don't choose) to put in writing, and whether or not they put anything in writing at all. In this, I realize that some women who view as unnecessary the clausal stipulation allowing a woman her own Islamic fiqh view, do in fact uphold the Sunnah of having a written contract. However, they simply do not believe that this particular stipulation is necessary, wise, or even "Islamically correct." And that is their right, as all humans have the right to their own religious perspectives and conclusions (which, of course, is the whole point of the marriage clause itself, but I digress).

It is my experience, however, that most women who hold this passive (and inherently risky and self-effacing) point of view in the beginning of marriage—which is often rooted in a genuine belief that foregoing having the final say on equivocal religious matters related to her own spiritual practice is equivalent to submitting to the leadership of her husband—do not hold this same point of view years down the line. This shift in perspective is very often due mainly to their own emotional exhaustion and spiritual burnout. Or it is due to the natural emotional maturity and spiritual insight that come with age and experience. In other cases, this shift in perspective is due to a woman either intimately witnessing the spiritual crisis or abuse of women around her, or to hearing about an alarming number of these cases.

Nonetheless, I cannot in good conscience say that even these women should be *compelled* to stipulate this religious boundary in their marriage contract. Just as a woman has the right to place the stipulation in her contract if she so chooses, she also has the right to forgo it if she so chooses. So, it is true that not all women want or "need" this clause. But I would argue their souls need it, even if they don't.

Five

Are Women Property of Men?

In this chapter, I share one of the last texts I sent to the imam-therapist after our disagreement about a woman putting in her marriage contract that she can follow the Islamic opinion that she genuinely believes is most correct or safest for her soul in front of Allah. I've kept the texts exactly as I typed them at the time, except to edit for minor typos and to offer clarity in certain terminology (which I put in parentheses, though some of these parentheses were in the original text). I've broken up the texts into chapter sections with topic titles for clarity.

Does a Woman's Experience or Knowledge Matter?

So, I wanted to share this one last point on the topic we've been discussing about the woman's right to the ultimate decision for anything she feels will deeply affect her relationship with her soul:

Firstly, I believe my point of view can be best understood through experiential knowledge along with spiritual knowledge. However, in the ummah today, the experiential knowledge of women is generally devalued. Even if thousands of women have the same experience along with sincere *emaan*, all of that experience and *taqwaa* amounts to nothing next to the mere opinion of a man (with or without his own experiential or spiritual knowledge), especially if he carries the title "husband." I believe this is a sign of the Last Days, not reflective of our deen in truth.

Secondly, it is my belief that at the heart of the Qur'an and prophetic teachings is a spiritual way of life that grants every adult soul (male *and* female) not only the right to make any final decision that they sincerely believe will affect their soul, but also the obligation to do so. No authoritative relationship, whether between parent and adult child, scholar and worshipper, or husband and wife, has the divine authority to come between that.

If a husband sincerely feels his wife is wrong, he certainly has the "right" to use his leadership role to compel her to do what he believes is right, and in this transient worldly experience, she would be obliged to follow him (or at least she'll likely *feel* obligated to follow him). But it is my belief that in front of Allah, this man is committing a serious *dhulm* (wrongdoing) through which he is exposing himself to the risk of Hellfire.

This is because he is asking her to do something that she has already made clear to him that she genuinely feels will either harm her soul directly or will result in mental or emotional distress (even if the man doesn't understand exactly how). So, unless what she is doing is unequivocally *haraam* (forbidden) based on the texts in the Qur'an and Sunnah and is thus an issue of *ijmaa'* (full consensus amongst scholars with no other valid opinions historically) amongst the companions and the *salaf* (earliest Muslims), then he is behaving like an abuser toward his wife, even if he doesn't intend to and even if he imagines himself to be a "good man" looking out for the welfare of his family.

"Good Men" Cause the Most Harm

In these matters, self-proclaimed "good men" cause the most harm because they are blinded by their general compassion and empathetic nature, so they fall into *ghuroor* (personal and spiritual self-deception), which harms them and their loved ones.

The reason I mentioned the necessity to differentiate between a certain type of woman when examining the clause that I propose in the contract is this: A woman who is known to take her deen and mental health very seriously should not be treated like someone for whom religion "isn't that serious" or whose character or mindset suggests frivolity (even if it's sincere, "harmless" frivolity).

In my view, any man who does not have the humility and *baseerah* (insight) to understand the absolute necessity of the clause I mentioned for the former type of woman (especially if she herself is requesting it) is in danger of harming his own soul and the soul (and long-term mental health) of his wife and family. If this man sincerely wants to protect his wife from the Hellfire, he should educate himself on what this actually means; and aside from very clear sins and *shirk* (paganism) in the name of Islam, compulsion (i.e., pulling rank) is not generally part of encouraging others toward goodness and being saved from the Fire.

This Helped When I Almost Left Islam

Lastly, on a personal note. When I was at my lowest spiritually and dedicated myself to the deep study of Qur'an and the prophetic teachings as a means to save my soul, it was this single spiritual truth that made me appreciate my deen again and see the beauty of my faith in the context of marriage: **No matter what worldly role someone has over you, your soul remains forever your domain,** and your

Merciful Rabb has given you and you alone the final say in protecting the health of your soul.

My Spiritual Heartbreak Begins

For years, I've genuinely believed that any compassionate man with sincere *emaan* who feared Allah would think the same, especially with regards to the affairs of women in marriage. And this gave me an inkling of hope that the soul companionship of marriage can be good for my mental and spiritual health, as well as the mental and spiritual health of other women.

Today, I realize I was wrong.

Alhamdulillah, after our conversation, I still believe the same about my deen and my rights to decisions that affect my soul, especially in marriage. But I'm honestly saddened that sincere men of faith like yourself see this aspect of our deen very differently.

I know you agree "in principle" to most of what I said, but to me, the crux of the issue is that in the end, this agreement "in principle" is not strong enough to translate into fully supporting a believing woman in having that support put in *writing,* such that a believing man is obligated to honor it. So, in my view, that's the same as saying a man doesn't have to honor it; as in the end, his male authority—in official agreements—takes precedence over a woman's right to her own soul.

Are Women Property of Men?

In other words, without this *signed* agreement, it means a married woman *is,* in fact, in practical reality, the full property of her husband, in body, mind, and soul. She is his slave and his "prison ward" with only elusive rights that he bestows whenever his "good heart" feels so inclined.

Otherwise, (according to you and men who think like you) even her own soul is his property more than hers.

We can speak all day and night about what good men "should be" doing. But when good men are unwilling to put in *writing* what they say they should be doing, it means they don't really believe they are obligated to do it in the first place.

SubhaanAllaah.

Thus, the most important right that Allah gave all humans is officially denied to women for no other reason than she was born female and married a man she imagined would be at the forefront in protecting and honoring this most sacred right.

It's an eye-opening lesson for me, more than I can convey in words. But it does certainly clarify for me just how differently Islam is understood between men and women—and why so many of us as women remain in spiritual crisis, barely holding on to our *emaan*, feeling as if we have no official rights over anything of ours, not even our souls if a man decides we shouldn't.

If good men think like this, what hope is there for *any* Muslim woman in any marriage?

PART TWO

My Spiritual Heartbreak
Male Leadership in these
Last Days

"The most dangerous person in this world is the one who denies his own darkness, especially if he has also assigned himself the role of hero or savior who is fighting other people's darknesses... The more the self-proclaimed do-gooder hides his own darkness from himself, the more it spreads within him. But in the Qur'an and Sunnah, goodness and spiritual purity aren't claims on the tongue; they are standards on a path of striving for good. Yet amongst self-proclaimed 'good men,' their savior complex afflicts them with the same grandiose ideology of 'good white people.' These are privileged men and women who genuinely imagine they're incapable of racism. Meanwhile, they are inflicting harm on the very lives and souls they claim to be protecting from harm and supporting in life—just like 'good men' do to women every day. And just like the tone deafness of 'good white people' incites them to disregard the perspective of any Black person that challenges them to self-correct—not only swoop down to 'save' and 'help'—so it is with 'good Muslim men.' These men pride themselves on being 'soldiers for good.' Yet their hero-savior complex has blinded them to the fact that there is no such thing as being a unilaterally 'good man.' There's no such thing as being someone who is always a source of good—except insomuch as you remain aware of your ever-present human inclination to also be a source of harm."

—from the journal of Umm Zakiyyah

Six

It Wasn't an Easy Decision

In the end, the imam-therapist called me "unsafe." His reasoning was two-fold: firstly, my point of view on a woman's right to her own spiritual practice being put in her marriage contract (which he viewed as wronging men), and secondly, my unwillingness to give *him* personal access to my female audience in a marriage-prep program idea I'd previously shared with him.

Before our fateful conversations about the woman's right to her own soul in marriage, I had considered appointing this imam-therapist as the head instructor and advisor in the Preliminary Wakeel Program (PWP) I'd devised. This was a marriage-prep program I had designed to help women in vulnerable situations, specifically those who were seeking marriage but didn't have much (or any) help or support from male relatives.

Naturally, after my last interactions with the imam-therapist (the dark details of which I won't even get into for this book, but this was when he made his Muslim male-supremacist ideology undeniably clear, and unapologetically so), I couldn't betray these women's trust like that. I couldn't expose my clients and students to *known* emotional and spiritual harm, no matter how badly I wanted the PWP program to go forward.

However, in the mind of this male supremacist imam-therapist, I was wronging *him* with this boundary. He felt I was betraying his trust by making the necessary (though difficult) decision to pause the program until I could find a suitable replacement. Though I'd only *vocalized* my idea to him and said I was considering asking him to head it, he felt that our conversations alone about my idea meant I was beholden to him.

I Couldn't Go Forward

Ultimately, as heartbreaking as it was at the time, I realized I couldn't go forward with the PWP marriage-prep program with him as the head. Instead, I had to find a replacement. I needed to appoint as head of this program a man who believed in prophetic masculinity, not the hyper-masculinity of the Red Pill cult. I needed to appoint as head a sincere man of taqwaa who followed the prophetic Sunnah of compassionate masculinity. This was the type of manhood rooted in the soul-centered Islamic model of religion—divine supremacy—instead of the man-centered Western model of religion: male supremacy.

Today, the search for the head of this program continues.

This is because in these Last Days, it is far more common for a Muslim man, even amongst our most celebrated scholars and spiritual teachers, to uphold male supremacy over divine supremacy.

As a result, it is on this male-centric foundation that most Muslim men build their understanding of *qawwaamah* (Islamic manhood), of religious scholarship, and of their own divinely assigned spiritual leadership in the homes and in the community. As such, most men in these Last Days rarely (if ever) rely on the prophetic example of taqwaa-centered manhood in truth.

This compassionate, prophetic leadership is rooted in divine supremacy, which prioritizes the health of the human soul (male and female) above all else in this transient world.

Seven

Why Are We Taught Islam Like This?

Today, we're taught Islam through the lens of male supremacy. In the practical reality of life for Muslim women, this means that any woman who chooses to practice her faith based on divine supremacy (i.e., based on the Qur'an and prophetic Sunnah) is swiftly labeled "feminist" in the most derogatory sense. Or she is subjected to all sorts of other slanderous insults, personal attacks, and verbal abuse—sometimes even bodily harm.

This is because she committed the most unforgivable sin that a woman can fall into in the religion of male supremacy: She centered Allah over men, thereby choosing the health and wellness of her own soul over the demands, desires, and opinions of men.

In shock and indignant righteousness, male supremacists then rush to podcast mics to tell the world what a horrible "low value" woman she is.

Red Pill Podcasts Are Just the Beginning

It is well known that male-centered men (and women), especially those heavily influenced by male supremacist extremist cults like Red Pill, use podcast mics to spread their

43

misogyny and performative masculinity. However, in the Muslim community, it reaches much farther than that.

In our faith community, Muslim male supremacists use conference microphones during Islamic events. They use the masjid pulpit on Fridays during the Jumu'ah sermon. They use social media platforms like Instagram and TikTok. They also upload long YouTube video rants—often under the guise of fighting feminism, but really, their anti-feminism rhetoric is just the cover story. **Their real aim is to silence and vilify *any* Muslim woman who has the audacity to love herself enough outside the context of centering men.** This is especially the case if she has taken very real steps to protect herself from *their* harm (e.g., a divorced woman living in contentment after leaving a toxic or abusive marriage).

The Problem Is Always Us or Some External Phantom

When we seek to upgrade our standards for marriage for the sake of our well-being, this is a problem. When we seek to heal in solitude for the sake of our mental and spiritual health, this is a problem. When we choose to walk away from abusive relationships to protect our safety—and to preserve our spiritual relationships with Allah—this is a problem.

On and on, in the eyes of our "leaders" who practice Islam based on male supremacy instead of divine supremacy, the problem is almost "out there" somewhere. So, they blame feminism, Western culture, the high divorce rate, single mothers, women's "unrealistic expectations," women's ingratitude, career women, independent women, women getting an education, and on and on...

But **almost never do these "leaders" see *themselves* as the LEADERS in the problems afflicting the ummah and the world today.** Meanwhile, our Muslim lands are being destroyed. Innocent men, women, and children are dying in genocides. Believers worldwide are being tortured and persecuted in unimaginable ways.

Why? Because most Muslim men of today—even amongst our imams, scholars, and spiritual teachers—fixate on their inherent "superiority" over women more than on their inherent obligations to their own souls, to the women under their care, or to the ummah at large. As a result, they fixate on what women owe *them* vs. what they owe women— or even what they own their own lives and souls in front of Allah.

They Think Manhood = Entitlement

For this reason, so many Muslim men genuinely imagine that their divinely granted "superiority" is primarily about their relationship with women and their endless entitlement to female submission and sacrifice—even when a woman doesn't want a relationship with them anymore.

This, instead of recognizing that **their divine assignment of** *qawwaamah* **(male leadership)—which they love to call "superiority"—is about their relationship with Allah and their own souls.** It's also about their obligation *toward* women. It's about their obligation to sacrifice in Allah's cause.

It's not about men having a divine right to endless sacrifices and servitude of women for their own pleasure and egos.

The submission, obedience, and respect men are granted from women by Allah are in *response* to their fulfillment of their obligations. It is not an inherent birthright entitling men to female service because of their Y chromosome.

However, since in these Last Days, most Muslim men— including our ignorant "leaders"—have chosen the Western model of religion (i.e., male supremacy) over the Islamic model of religion (i.e, divine supremacy), they can't *see* themselves. Consequently, they keep blaming everything and everyone else for their own problems. So, they blame "bad women" and feminism. They blame alimony and the West. They blame independent women and the high divorce rate. On and on.

Weak Leaders Waiting for Strong Women to Lead

Meanwhile, as they call themselves leaders, they refuse to see anything in the mirror except their "superior" reflections. So, they claim to need "good, submissive women" to show up and act as conduits of their manhood in marriage. This, before they can fully carry out the weighty mission that God has assigned them in this world.

In other words, these "superior men" feel incapable of showing up as real men until we show up as "real women" on their behalf. In this way, they see women as the stronger, more capable gender. They also see us as the more natural leaders in this world.

However, they *claim* their obsession with needing a "submissive woman" just means they need us to show up for them first because our servitude to them somehow "activates" their inner masculinity. But that's just another way of saying the same thing. If you need someone else to show up for you before you can show up for yourself or the world, then *they* are the natural leader, not you.

In this way, deep down, male supremacists believe the very things they *claim* Western feminists believe: Women hold all the power, not men, so the world is much better off with assigning women as leaders instead of men. Apparently, the Red Pill cult agrees with this ideology because they say all these non-traditional, feminist women are blocking their manhood—as they (allegedly) have no access to their own masculinity unless we show up as conduits on their behalf.

The Darkness of Today's World Is Men's Handiwork

Tragically, male supremacist men simply don't see their own inner darkness and cowardice for what it is. They don't see that their lack of manhood is self-inflicted. They don't see how their own spiritual weakness is at the source of their problems. They don't see how their own collective wounded masculinity, which is rooted in generations of unhealed emotional wounds, is overtaking their lives, minds, and souls—just as it is overtaking the world.

Consequently, they don't see their own cowardice, weakness, and darkness of the *nafs* (inner self) for the collective and personal shortcoming that it is. Instead, they see everyone else's shortcomings as the problem. This is because all of their cowardice, weakness, and darkness is carefully hidden behind their frantic, desperate claims of male superiority and "high value" manhood. Meanwhile, these "strong, superior men" wait anxiously for *women* to show up for them before they feel capable enough to show up as real men.

And the result? The world we all live in.

Need proof? Just look around you. This is the world created by all the "high value men" and "natural born leaders." These "strong leaders" are shouting ad nauseam into podcast mics and are uploading new YouTube videos almost every day about the problems and faults of women who are (allegedly) too blind or unrighteous to submit to their leadership.

Meanwhile, nearly every continent these men touch and stake "leadership" on is ravaged by oppression, genocide, wars, misogyny, abuse, and more darkness and evil than you can name.

This is their handiwork.

This is the work of our male leadership today.

Yet still, they're looking to women to come and save them. And since so many of us are running from them (and rightfully so), then apparently, we are to blame for the state of the world, not them.

Eight

We Tried So Hard to Support Our Men

It's true that when it comes to the collective problems afflicting the world in these Last Days, both men and women carry a portion of the blame. However, due to men's unique divine assignment of leadership (which so many of them prefer to call "superiority"), the heaviest responsibility for the state of today's world is on the shoulders of those carrying the "superior" role of leadership.

Unfortunately, however, so many of our men would rather cling to the entitled victimhood of male supremacy (where they can blame others and claim to be an oppressed gender whose superiority isn't recognized as it should) over the weighty *amaanah* (divine trust and responsibility) of divine supremacy (where they can only blame themselves and then humbly accept the divine call to true manhood, which is rooted in taqwaa and self-accountability).

What About the Marriage Crisis?

That women are running away from male supremacist men en masse (and at younger and younger ages) isn't the source of the problem.

It's a symptom.

The source of the problem is our men's own dark, unhealed nafs (inner self), which makes it increasingly unwise and unsafe—emotionally, psychologically, spiritually, and physically—to be in their company, let alone in a long-term intimate relationship with them.

So yes, no matter what share of the blame women also carry in today's "marriage crisis," the main source of this problem, especially as it relates to droves of women running from marriage and men, is men's own individual and collective abandonment of their own wellness, safe presence, and personal integrity. **It is men's individual and collective abandonment of sincere humility, of self-correction, of principled protection of women (instead of obsessive control of them), and their abandonment of the prophetic Sunnah of compassionate leadership and manhood rooted in taqwaa** (i.e., God-consciousness, self-discipline, and self-accountability).

It is men's abandonment of prophetic masculinity. It is men's addiction to entitled masculinity. It is men's obsession with male supremacy over divine supremacy. It is men's unhealed hearts that are filled with love of Red Pill cult ideology, of unconditional feminine servitude, and of performative hyper-masculinity.

This is the source of the problem.

Are You Ready to Actually Lead?

We can't have it both ways. Men can't be the leaders at home and in society while *also* seeing women as both the main problem and solution to the marriage crisis today.

This isn't intended as a diss or as an ad hominem attack on men. It's a call to action. How so? Because if men's inaction is at the root of the problem, then it also means that men actively showing up as real men of taqwaa is the solution to the problem.

This is the price of leadership in the world. It doesn't apply only when things are going in your favor and your ego is being stroked. It also applies (and even more so) when the whole world looks like it's falling apart, when it seems everyone is against you, and when you feel everyone is blaming you and broadcasting your faults.

No, this doesn't mean men's feelings don't matter or that they don't have the right to hurt, feel offended, or even cry. Men are human beings just like women are human beings. So, these natural human reactions to emotional pain and frustration are to be expected. They're also signs of life in the human soul. These reactions mean that deep inside, this man is still "alive" somewhere, and that this topic of men's collective loss of manhood matters to him on a visceral level. So, on the whole, these human reactions are good things— as long as our men don't *live* in this place of hurt and frustration.

Manhood Is an Inside Job

No matter how we see men's and women's individual and collective challenges and darknesses in these Last Days, here's the bottom line: Becoming a real man of taqwaa is an inside job. No amount of female submission, self-erasure, restless obedience, and exhaustive self-sacrifice can make a man become a man.

Though so many of us—amongst men *and* women— have been taught otherwise.

This is something that I myself wish I'd known before signing up for marriage in these End Times. Growing up, I was taught that my loving feminine presence can make a man grow into a man, and I believed it.

I wish I'd learned, instead, what I myself needed to feel safe and loved and fully provided for in my feminine. This, before I rushed to the hamster wheel of exhaustive self-erasure and continuous sacrifice and shrinking on the altar of performative womanhood.

Yes, it's true. A compassionate, feminine presence can *help* a man. But it cannot *jumpstart* manhood in the life and heart of a man who isn't already invested in his own personal growth. It can only nurture masculine evolution in the heart of a man who is already actively moving in the right direction.

This is because, by nature, **manhood is internal and divinely gifted.** As such, a man's masculinity must be *individually* nurtured. These are the bottom lines, no matter what's happening in the world or in a man's personal life.

In other words, if you're a man, then you're tasked with showing up as a real man of taqwaa on your *own* behalf—and at all times. This, even if none of the women around you or even in your own home are showing up as "righteous wives" or as "good women" by *your* standards.

Otherwise, there can be no safety or relief from oppression in this world. Period.

For centuries, women have known this. And we've *tried* to tell our men. Sometimes we spoke these sentiments directly, sometimes we spoke them indirectly. But almost always, we spoke through our ever-present feminine submission, our exhaustive self-sacrifice, and our endless over-giving.

But still, our men wouldn't listen.

They dismissed us and called our efforts nagging. They withdrew from us and told us about man caves. They reminded us that men need silence and servitude. They told us we have a limited (or no) capacity to understand or respect what a man *really* needs.

They grew frustrated with us and shut us out. And so very often, they abandoned us and sought refuge in the arms (and bed) of another woman.

Yet still, we didn't give up on them.

We've Tried Soooo Hard to Support Them

We read zillions of books on femininity and womanhood. We signed up for marriage classes and "wife schools." We hired marriage coaches and begged advice from friends and elders. We sat on the couches of therapists and interrogated childhood wounds. We blamed ourselves for the faults and poor choices of our men. We meditated and prayed on how to be better partners and wives.

We've tried lowering our standards, giving up our rights, and choosing struggle love over our own comfort. We've tried supporting our men through poverty and joblessness. We've tried forgiving their private and public sins—and even pardoning their abuse, infidelity, and unkindness.

We've tried supporting polygyny.

We've tried self-erasing and sacrificing.

We've tried hiding our pain and smiling wide in their presence—even when they were the ones hurting us.

We've tried *loving* these men into manhood.

We've offered up our bodies, minds, and souls as conduits of their masculinity.

Then we performed femininity until our nervous systems shut down. We served and obeyed and submitted until our bodies were exhausted into life-threatening illnesses.

We birthed their children with no guarantee of a present father (even while we were still married). We buried children and loved ones and woke up days (or hours) later cooking and cleaning and servicing and pleasuring our men.

ANYTHING to awaken "the man within."

ANYTHING to help our men to *become* men.

ANYTHING to save our men, our marriages, and our ummah from ruin.

ANYTHING to restore true manhood to this world.

But to no avail.

Then, after all of this, **they blame us for not being small enough.**

Nine

Does Allah Hate Women? She Asked

I was shocked. It was the worst possible thing you could say out loud, asking something like that. And yet she'd asked it. She did more than ask, actually. She shared it as a statement of how she genuinely felt at the moment. But her tone, at least in how I received it, was a heartfelt plea to all of us on that Muslim Reddit forum.

She wanted to be wrong. She was begging us to tell her she was wrong. And almost all the Muslims there told her just that. But not in an attempt to help her work through her dark feelings, but in an attempt to shame her for having them in the first place. Or worst still, for expressing them out loud.

I didn't respond. Not because I didn't want to. But because I couldn't. I had no words for it.

But amidst all the "you should be ashamed for saying this!" comments, there was one kind soul who said she'd gone through the same spiritual crisis, and she shared how she worked through it. Reading this compassionate, patient response—for which even the original poster openly expressed gratitude—I cried.

I cried so much I started shaking. I cried so much I could barely breathe. I cried so much that I feared I would pass out. Why?

Because I'd never before seen such simple kindness shown to a Muslim woman who was hurting so badly and drowning so deeply. I'd only seen pain and suffering thrown on top of her already present pain and suffering. I'd only seen a woman shamed for feeling exactly how male supremacy had taught her to feel—about herself and her Lord.

I cried, wishing someone had extended the same simple kindness to me, even as my spiritual darkness never reached the level where I asked what she asked.

But I did begin to feel that Allah's male servants felt the way about me and other women that she feared Allah felt about us. And in a way, my feeling was just as confusing as hers. So, for years, I was left wondering things I could never speak out loud. But I did finally break down when I couldn't take it anymore, and I said my "dark truths" in a series of prayers, complaining to no one but Allah:

Aren't they supposed to be protecting us from harm? Why are they inflicting harm on us instead? What did we do to deserve this? What did I do?

Is it because You're displeased with me, O Allah?

If so, help me be a better woman, a better wife, and a better servant of Yours. And I beg You to protect me from the evil within myself!

And O Allah, I beseech You! Help me understand.

Why do Your male servants hate us so much? Why do they get so much joy out of our pain?

O Allah! Forgive me for asking. I'm not trying to be disrespectful, but forgive me if I am. For You know our hearts better than we know our own. But I really don't understand. And maybe I don't even have the right to ask. But please help me get through this, O Allah! Help me find the answers I need for my soul. I just want to understand my faith, O Allah. And I just want to understand myself.

I just want to die as a believer, O Allah. I just want meet You with emaan in my heart. And now, with all these darknesses that I'm carrying, I fear that I won't.

I want to know, is this my religion? Or is this just my test in this world? Or is it true what they say about us? That people like me are mainly fodder for Your Hellfire? Then men like them are Your most beloved and guaranteed homes in Your Paradise? If so, please protect me from the Fire, O Allah! Even if I deserve it. And please forgive me for the sins I know I've fallen into, and the sins I don't even remember committing. And forgive me for the sins I can't bring myself to fully repent from because in my heart, I'm not fully sorry for having done them at all. But I beg You to help me to want to <u>want</u> the good, even when I'm doing bad.

But, O Allah, forgive me, I must share what's on my heart. So, I ask You with a heart that is breaking, a soul that is hurting, and a body that is exhausted and barely holding on to life: Why did you assign as our protectors in this world people who only wish us harm? Why did you assign as our protectors in this world men who only want to protect themselves? And, O Allah! Help me understand. For I truly do not know. How am I supposed to stay safe in this world when I have to protect myself from the very people you assigned as my protectors?

Ten

Are We Really *That* Bad? I Wondered

I think one of the hardest things to work through after living life through the lens of male supremacy is detoxing from what it teaches you about yourself and other female souls. I don't know how this affects other women exposed to male supremacist darkness. But I know it left me feeling worthless and dehumanized.

Yet male supremacists tell us not to worry about that, because all we need to do is find a hero-savior "superior" man who wants to marry us. Then he (and only he) can act as our source of worthiness and humanity in this world. However, they don't hesitate to remind us that we can only benefit from this "amazing blessing of marriage" if we fully commit to making this man an intermediary between us and Allah. Because, as the imam-therapist told me, that's their entire job as heads of household, to make all our spiritual decisions on our behalf.

This is because, apparently, according to male supremacists, Allah doesn't accept the worship of a married woman unless her husband has approved of it first. So, this "superior man"—even if he himself barely prays or reads the Qur'an—is supposed to be, on behalf of my "inferior female soul," micromanaging my private relationship with Allah.

And if I don't let him (i.e., submit to him as my spiritual authority over Allah), then *I'm* in sin even while I'm praying or doing any other good deed.

This is because, for married women in male supremacy, it isn't *ikhlaas* (spiritual sincerity) that is the foundation of your goodness and piety, and even of your good deeds being accepted. It is pleasing your husband. And only after you've pleased this man does Allah pay any attention to you. Before that, not even your sincerity or taqwaa holds much weight.

Did I Misunderstand My Religion All This Time?

Personally, after enduring years of this type of spiritual self-erasure and hearing over and over how horrible and deficient we are as women…

After years of listening to sheikhs and imams say ad nauseam how we as women are the majority of Hellfire…

After hearing over and over again—even from the cruelest and most abusive of men—how *they* are superior to us… So, it doesn't matter how cruelly they treat us. It doesn't matter how sincere we are to Allah. It doesn't matter how loving we are to them. They come out on top, always.

After enduring all this religious harm day after day, I found myself wondering, *"What's the point of all of this? Is there any point to all of this?"*

I just couldn't make sense of it.

I even began to wonder if I'd misunderstood my faith all along. *Maybe Islam is exactly as all those "Islamophobic" anti-religion atheists and other non-Muslims claim*, I considered, distraught.

But I fought those thoughts and feelings.

At least I *tried* to.

Yet they'd always find a way back into the darknesses of my *nafs*. Then, over time, it felt like they *became* the darkness of my nafs. So, I saw no way out of the waves of darkness overtaking me and drowning me, pulling me away from my faith. So, naturally, when I was at my lowest, I felt like I could no longer be Muslim.

But even after I worked through *that*, I still wasn't okay. This is because I was struggling to believe that I even *mattered* to Allah or that He loved me.

Or that I even had a right to love myself.

Make It Make Sense

Male supremacy had taught me so many things, and not a single one of them left me feeling like I had a single thing of value to offer this world. I was left feeling like my presence alone brought nothing except darkness and perpetual harm to the earth.

I was left feeling like, by virtue of being a female soul, I was afflicted with incorrigible ingratitude, even if I were gifted lasting love in marriage. That I was cursed with irreparable female deficiency, even if I dedicated my entire life to sincerely worshipping Allah and obeying Him.

There was no way out of the abyss, I felt at the time.

Then there were all those teachings that male supremacists taught that I just couldn't make sense of, that I couldn't reconcile with foundational things I knew from the Qur'an.

On the one hand, male supremacy teaches us that the Qur'an is the source of foundational truth and that everything else from our faith must be filtered through this foundational lens. This is also something that divine supremacy teaches, as from an Islamic perspective, it's absolutely true.

But then, on the other hand, male supremacy teaches us to completely ignore what the Qur'an says when it comes to who is the majority of the Hellfire and why. They also teach us to ignore what the Qur'an says about the worst possible sin.

In the Qur'an, the majority of the Hellfire are disbelievers, and it is *kufr* (disbelief) that is the worst of sins. But in male supremacy, the majority of the Hellfire are women, and the worst of sins is a woman's ingratitude to her husband. (Now, keep in mind, many of them will recite on their tongues that *shirk* is the worst sin. But then they'll turn around and spiritual abuse women into committing *shirk* with them, thereby forcing her to override what she sincerely believes is *halaal* and *haraam* in front of Allah to follow them. In this, they are like the modern-day Christians who claim on their tongues to believe in monotheism, but they make paganism a requirement of faith by saying people must worship Prophet Jesus, peace be upon him, as God).

"Both Can Be True!" They Say

I get it. I can do the math.

What do I mean? Because many *women* are disbelievers. So, both things can be true.

I've considered this explanation, and more than once. In fact, many nights while in the throes of spiritual crisis, I lay awake trying to make it all make sense. *Maybe this is talking about disbelieving women?*

But there was only one problem. So, I thought: *But wait…how can that be?*

After all, Islam teaches that *kufr* is a sin that overtakes all other sins, thus making every other sin practically irrelevant in comparison. This doesn't mean disbelievers won't be punished for their other sins. It just means that when placed next to their sins of *kufr* or *shirk* (worshipping other than Allah), there is absolutely no sin that is worse by comparison.

What does this mean in practical reality in the Hereafter?

It means that when someone comes on the Day of Judgment having died upon *kufr* or *shirk*, then their lesser sins won't be the cause of their *worst* punishment. It won't be what's causing them to fill up Hellfire in droves.

It is only Muslims whose worst sin can possibly be something other than *kufr*. This brings us back to the sin of ingratitude to our husbands, a sin that is almost always spoken of in the context of how *Muslim women* treat their spouses.

But in the Qur'an and Sunnah, we're taught that as a whole, Muslim men and women will be the minority of all of humankind on the Day of Judgment. There's even a hadith that says out of every 1000 people in existence, 999 will enter the Hellfire. Then we're told that the majority of these are Gog and Magog, so as to not distress us.

This brings us back to the dilemma of teaching Muslim women that *they* are the majority of the Hellfire. Yet they are neither disbelievers nor amongst the Gog and Magog, at least not any Muslim women of today.

So, if we take this narration at face value, based on the foundational evidences from the Qur'an, along with other supplemental prophetic narrations about the Hereafter, then the way I understand it is that the *most* we can claim is this: This is talking about disbelieving women who *combine* their unforgivable sin of *kufr* with the lesser sin of ingratitude to their husbands.

As for Muslim women, their sins fall into the category of all other sins committed by the children of Adam (male and female) who believe in Allah and the Last Day: Some of them will fall into the lesser sin of ingratitude to their husbands. Thus, as is the case for all sins committed by Muslims, some of these women will be forgiven for this, while others won't.

Either way, even if the believing women who *aren't* forgiven for this sin are numerous beyond our comprehension, it's simply not possible to conclude what we've been taught: that ungrateful Muslim wives, as a whole, make up the majority of the inhabitants of Hellfire. This would require them to outnumber the disbelievers, and that's simply not possible.

And if the meaning is meant to include disbelievers in this number too, then are male supremacists always saying this to believing women, as if it's mainly *their* reality being spoken about here?

"But We Shouldn't Take This Lightly!"

Don't get me wrong. I understand that no sin is trivial in front of Allah, and we should take no sin lightly.

I also realize that no matter how many or few people are punished for any particular sin on the Day of Judgment, not a single one of us should trivialize that sin in this world. Most significantly, for the sake of our souls, none of us should feel safe from *any* sin deserving of punishment in the Hereafter.

So, my point isn't to say this sin isn't serious. My point is simply this: Given all the *other* evidences from our faith about what *also* happens in the Hereafter, many of which are directly related to the topic being discussed here many of which are more established and unequivocal than this one (i.e., disbelievers being the majority of the Hellfire), why is so much emphasis, so much time, and so much energy spent on quoting this narration as if it's more foundational than everything about Paradise and Hellfire put together?

So, what's really going on here?

It would be years later that a friend of mine shared a simple explanation that settled in all in my mind: This hadith is speaking about one segment of Hellfire, not the entirety of Hellfire itself. In some segments of Hellfire, men are the majority, in others women, and so on.

Honestly, till today, that's the only explanation that makes sense to my heart and soul. At the same time, I realize there's so much I don't know about this *ghayb* (unseen reality). So, I fully acknowledge that Allah is the best knower of what will happen to His slaves on the Last Day.

My prayer is that whatever happens, I will be protected from harm and punishment.

Which is why, till today, I remain committed to leaving alone the idol of male supremacy and instead worshipping Allah alone for the sake of my soul.

PART THREE

Who Is Your Lord?
The Idol of Male Supremacy

"In male supremacy, the lives, minds, and souls of women are controlled by the men in their lives, most especially their husbands. So, we as women have no right to our own life paths, our own independent thought, or even our own spiritual practice. This is because male supremacists consider any female autonomy as equal to religious misguidance or Western feminism. Thus, men are given full responsibility for (and authority over) every part of women's lives. Meanwhile, we're blocked from any responsibility or authority over our own lives. But there is one significant exception to this: when it lets men off the hook for what they've done to us when things go wrong.

In other words, we as women are fully responsible for our own lives, minds, and souls <u>only</u> when it absolves men of any accountability for what we suffered at their hands. But we were just trying to please Allah by centering men (even if we suffered as a result), as they told us we had to do. This is when they start blaming us for centering them, saying, 'Nobody forced her into that marriage!' or 'Nobody forced her to do such and such!' or (their favorite when running from accountability): 'Women need to take accountability for their own lives and choices!' Yet previously, when we did just that, we were slandered and dragged for not blindly trusting the decisions and demands of men."

—from the journal of Umm Zakiyyah

Eleven

Detoxing from Male Supremacist Shirk

For years, I had had no idea I was living my faith through the lens of male supremacy. In fact, I thought Islam *was* male supremacy. No, this wasn't a conscious thought process on my part. I didn't even know what male supremacy was, in fact. But that doesn't make its harms to me and my soul any less real.

When you realize that your subconscious is running your life far more than your conscious perceptions, then you can begin to understand how something like this can happen. I think, on some level, it happens to all of us, even outside the context of religion or male supremacy.

For me personally, everything I'd thought about myself as a Muslim woman was through the male supremacist lens, and I suffered mightily for it.

But the fact of the matter is, most of us are taught Islam through this lens, and we're *all* suffering as a result—even if we're not fully conscious of just how much.

What Is Male Supremacy Anyway?

You might be wondering what male supremacy is and how it's different from Islamic spirituality. After all, Allah did assign men as our leaders at home and in society, and He did grant men a degree of favor and responsibility over women.

But male supremacy isn't about recognizing a unique divine favor that Allah granted men. It's about denying the divine responsibility and accountability that comes along with this favor.

Most significantly, male supremacy is about shifting the focus of our faith from the supreme greatness of Allah (and every soul's responsibility to serve and please Him) to the "supreme" greatness of men (and every person's—especially a woman's—responsibility to serve and please them). **This results in viewing everything, whether our public and private acts of worship or our most intimate private choices in life and love, through a male-centric, "male superiority" lens.**

In other words, the foundational *'aqeedah* (belief system) of Islam is turned on its head. Thus, a man's divinely assigned role of leadership in this world is viewed not as obligatory servitude to the Creator in service to the greater good of His creation on earth. Rather, it is viewed as the obligation of Allah's servants (most especially female souls) to be in perpetual servitude to men in service to men's desires and egos—even at the price of women's health, spiritual wellness, and servitude to Allah.

Islamic Tawheed vs. Western Shirk

Historically and currently, male supremacy is the Western model of religion, whereas divine supremacy (i.e., Tawheed) has been the Islamic model of religion since the beginning of time, dating back to the pure spiritual practice of our father Adam and his wife.

Whenever people of faith have deviated from the divine supremacy of Tawheed (true, untainted monotheism), their misguided religious ideology would take on different iterations. Each of these variations would ultimately lead to *shirk* (paganism), even if, in the beginning, it had taken on ostensibly "innocent" forms or even ostensible goodness.

Here, it is important to note that the sin of *shirk* itself has different levels and types, ranging from various types of minor *shirk*, which is centering other than Allah in our intentions (which is a serious sin but does not cancel out a person's Islam) to various types of major *shirk*, which is worshipping other than Allah or assigning divine rights and attributes to His creation (which cancels out a person's *emaan* completely).

When a divinely assigned role (e.g., male leadership at home and in society, or a woman respecting the leadership of a man) is viewed as a person's entire purpose in life—as opposed to worshipping and serving Allah alone—the religion is no longer centered around the Creator. Rather, it is now centered around the creation.

This might seem like an insignificant, technical point describing two sides of the same coin. But it's not. In fact, this type of inverting of spiritual practice and priority from centering the Creator to centering the creation is the very essence of *shirk* on a fundamental level.

The only part of creation that is *always* centered when we are centering Allah is the human soul, as this is where our divine-centric spiritual practice takes root. This is why centering Allah is equal to centering the health of your soul. No other creation besides the soul has this right to take center stage in your life.

This is why the Islamic model of religion (i.e., divine supremacy) can be thought of as soul-centric, whereas the Western model of religion (i.e., male supremacy) can be described as man-centric. No matter the context or circumstance, in Islam, the soul (through serving Allah) is always prioritized; and no matter the context or circumstance, in male supremacy, serving a man is always prioritized. The former is Tawheed and the latter is *shirk*. They are not two sides of the same coin, they are direct opposites.

But Shouldn't We Obey Our Husbands?

This is a common question many Muslims ask in these discussions. It's not much different from the question, "But shouldn't we obey our parents?" or "Shouldn't we always honor our mothers?" And the answer to each of these questions is the same: Obeying and honoring someone isn't the same as centering our entire faith practice around them.

We obey the creation only in matters that don't ask us to disobey Allah or cause harm to our lives or souls. Believing that Islam is male-centered just because we have obligations to our husbands is little different from claiming that Islam is female-centric because we have obligations to our mothers, not to mention the high honor granted to mothers above most other creation in this world.

Outside the context of marriage, **a random man doesn't have authority over your life just because he's a man.** We are obligated to serve Allah at all times, not any human being. Even our obligation to obey Prophet Muhammad ﷺ is ultimately about our obligation to obey Allah. This is why we say **Islam is about centering Allah.** In practical reality, this means always centering the spiritual health of your soul, no matter what human being has rights over you at the time.

Thus, Islam is soul-centered, as our soul is obligated to be in constant submission to Allah, and **shifting that constant submission to any creation harms the soul.** Therefore, it is only Allah whom we obey and serve unconditionally. Obeying any human being, whether a parent, scholar, or spouse, *always* comes with conditions. However, male supremacy shames and guilts women into believing that their life purpose is to be in servitude to a man unconditionally, especially in the context of marriage.

This ideology is *shirk*.

Twelve

They Say Islam Is Male-Centered

Whenever religious misguidance is first unfolding, it is "minor" and thoroughly justified through logical arguments (e.g., *"Centering men just means women should obey their husbands"*), so it is often viewed as good and praiseworthy, or even as a religious obligation in the eyes of people. This is especially the case when truth is mixed with falsehood, as it almost always is in cases of *bid'ah* (religious innovation) and *shirk*. This is why male supremacists love to highlight women's obligations to men in marriage. This is aimed at bolstering their arguments that "prove" Islam itself is male-centered. However, you'll notice that **the claims never stop at marriage.**

This is why single and divorced women get so much of their attention, even though marriage itself isn't obligatory in Islam. It's also why women who are content in unmarried solitude or are helping women avoid (or escape) abusive marriages enrage male supremacists. It's also why women who are seeking marriage but have a single boundary or standard for themselves that a random man cannot (or will not) meet are accused of having "unrealistic expectations" or "ridiculously high standards." In this context, it's important to understand this psychology:

Male supremacist men want (and demand) unlimited, unmitigated access to women without boundaries or conditions. Thus, any woman who doesn't grant this access—or who has a belief system (or healthy self-love) that tells her she isn't obligated to grant this access or who is reminding women they don't have to be guilted or shamed into an unwanted marriage or that women don't have to engage in self-erasure while pursuing marriage—is vilified, slandered, and subjected to all sorts of harm and harassment.

Additionally, it is almost always the case that this woman's religion, intentions, and integrity are called into question. This is where male supremacists often resort to their favorite silencing, vilification tool: calling a Muslim woman a "feminist," but in the derogatory anti-Islamic sense of the term (not in the "women should be treated like full human beings" sense of the term). Here, it doesn't matter whether or not the woman herself identifies as a feminist (more on that later, *inshaa'Allah*). **The goal is simply to discredit, silence, and vilify.**

In other words, in this moment, the goal of the male supremacist is exactly the same as the "patriotic" white supremacist Islamophobe calling a law-abiding Muslim citizen a terrorist. They know the effect it's going to have on their audience, and that's the point. So, the truth doesn't really matter in this case because **the goal isn't truth-telling; it is inflicting the maximum amount of harm and irreparable damage.** It's also about using this person as a lesson and a cautionary tale to anyone else who dares to follow their path.

In the context of a divorced woman dedicating her life to giving women the skills to protect themselves from harm, the goal of the "cautionary tale" social lynching by male supremacists is to shame currently married abused women into staying in unsafe, dangerous relationships.

This is because male supremacist men are not the least bit invested in keeping women safe from harm or protecting women at all. **They are invested in keeping themselves safe from accountability and protecting their egos (and each other) at all times**. They believe it is their divine right to own, control, and harm women, and to even have access to the bodies and lives of women who do not even want to marry them (or stay married to them).

In the Qur'an, Allah warns men against this male-centered psychology of "I have the right to women even if they don't want me!" or "I can mistreat them as I like!" when He says:

يَـٰٓأَيُّهَا ٱلَّذِينَ ءَامَنُوا لَا يَحِلُّ لَكُمْ أَن تَرِثُوا ٱلنِّسَآءَ كَرْهًا وَلَا تَعْضُلُوهُنَّ لِتَذْهَبُوا بِبَعْضِ مَآ ءَاتَيْتُمُوهُنَّ إِلَّآ أَن يَأْتِينَ بِفَٰحِشَةٍ مُّبَيِّنَةٍ وَعَاشِرُوهُنَّ بِٱلْمَعْرُوفِ فَإِن كَرِهْتُمُوهُنَّ فَعَسَىٰٓ أَن تَكْرَهُوا شَيْئًا وَيَجْعَلَ ٱللَّهُ فِيهِ خَيْرًا كَثِيرًا ﴿١٩﴾

"O you who have believed, it is not lawful for you to inherit women by compulsion. And do not make difficulties for them in order to take [back] part of what you gave them unless they commit a clear immorality. And live with them in kindness. For if you dislike them - perhaps you dislike a thing and Allah makes therein much good."
—*An-Nisaa* (4:19)

Their male-centered psychology is also why women who do not ostensibly "need" a man—either because they are financially self-sufficient due to Allah's *qadar* or because they

74

are living in calm *tawakkul* and contentment while unmarried—are accused of being "non-traditional" women or "masculine" independent women (in the most derogatory sense of the term).

So, yes, male supremacist men absolutely do want women to center them in all matters of love and faith. But that's not all. **They also want women to be utterly incapable of living without them.** They also want to block and shame women from feeling they even have the right (or option) to access *halaal* contentment or happiness outside the context of serving and centering men at all times.

Thirteen

Man-Centered vs. Soul-Centered Love and Faith

In male supremacy, the unique needs, psychology, desires, personal circumstances, or even the God-given rights of women are rarely (if ever) prioritized or even seriously considered. This is especially the case if a woman's unique needs or rights will inconvenience a man, will grant the woman the right to say no to him for marriage, will allow a woman to dissolve a marriage with him, or will require him to "level up" as a real man of taqwaa in her presence.

Why? Because in male supremacy, only the needs, desires, and unique circumstances of the man are used as a measuring stick for right and wrong—and *halaal* and *haraam*—in women's choices. This is why male supremacists are constantly insisting that women lower their standards for marriage, regardless of why she herself set that standard in the first place.

It's also why male supremacists are constantly insisting that women cannot divorce for "trivial" reasons. They know that by making this claim, a woman's life, mind, and soul are automatically put on trial—until she can prove to *them* that her reason isn't trivial, even if it was never trivial to Allah (as the quiet suffering of *any* of His servants is no small matter), even if no other human soul in this world (besides the woman herself) understands what she is going through.

To the male supremacist, nearly <u>all</u> reasons for a woman divorcing a man are trivial (or are cast into the category of "divorcing for no reason") in their eyes—that is, unless the man himself no longer wants the woman in his life, even if he himself doesn't have a reason other than wanting a brand new female body to keep him warm at night.

It's also why when male supremacists defend their vilification of women's "too high" standards for marriage, they almost always say something like, "Marriage should be made easy for the people!" thereby invoking the Sunnah of simplicity in seeking matrimony. However, interestingly, in proclaiming the need for marriage to be easy **for people**, they almost always erase from the meaning of "people" all human beings except men. This is because in their minds, women are not even considered "people" when upholding *any* Sunnah that grants humans access to Allah's unlimited favors of mercy, ease, and empathy.

So, Are We to Worship Men Now?

By the time any religious misguidance, such as male supremacy, reaches the level of major *shirk*, it has already become widespread and socially acceptable in a society or faith community. In this way, it has become completely fair-seeming to the people, even amongst the most intelligent of them.

In the Qur'an, Allah says:

$$ وَزَيَّنَ لَهُمُ ٱلشَّيْطَانُ أَعْمَالَهُمْ فَصَدَّهُمْ عَنِ ٱلسَّبِيلِ وَكَانُوا۟ مُسْتَبْصِرِينَ ﴿٣٨﴾ $$

> **"...And Shaytaan (Satan) made their deeds fair-seeming to them, and turned them away from the [right] Path, though they were gifted with intelligence and skill."**
> —*Al-'Ankaboot* (29:38)

Let's go back to something I mentioned at the beginning of the book: the imam-therapist's opinion that the entire role of men being "head of household" is to make all the spiritual decisions on a woman's behalf. Thus, (according to him), a woman shouldn't be allowed to have a personal relationship with Allah and her soul that her husband doesn't control or dictate. For this reason, a woman shouldn't have the right to follow the Islamic point of view that she genuinely believes is most correct in front of Allah or healthiest for her soul.

Now, remember when I mentioned in an earlier chapter how male supremacists will almost always mention the *role* of women in marriage (which comes with limits and conditions) and try to turn it into a woman's *life purpose* in both love and faith (with no limits or conditions)? Well, that's what is happening here. It's also how *'ebaadah* (worship) of Allah in a space of Tawheed can be easily and quickly turned into *'ebaadah* of men in a space of *shirk*.

If we believe the imam-therapist and other male supremacist men, religious leaders, marriage coaches, and relationship "experts," then in Islam, a woman is *obligated* to worship her husband. How so?

In the Qur'an, Allah says:

اَتَّخَذُوٓاْ أَحْبَارَهُمْ وَرُهْبَـٰنَهُمْ أَرْبَابًا مِّن دُونِ ٱللَّهِ

> **"They have taken their scholars [or rabbis and priests] and monks as lords besides Allah..."**
> —*At-Tawbah* (9:31)

It is narrated in a famous hadith that when 'Adee ibn Haatim, a prophetic Companion who had converted to Islam from Christianity, heard this *ayah* being recited, he said to the Prophet (peace be upon him): "We didn't worship them." The Prophet ﷺ responded, "Did they not make *haraam* (forbidden) what Allah had made *halaal* (permissible) and you made it *haraam* [too]? And did they not make *halaal* what Allah had made *haraam*, and you made it *halaal* [too]?" 'Adee replied, "Certainly." The Prophet ﷺ said, "That was how you worshipped them" (Al-Tirmidhi).

Therefore, when a woman is told she must abandon what she believes is *haraam* to follow what her husband believes is *halaal* or that she must abandon what she believes is *halaal* to follow what her husband believes in *haraam*, then according to the religion of Islam—which is based on divine supremacy, not male supremacy—she is being asked to worship her husband and take him as a god besides Allah, literally. This is the worst type of *shirk*, and it takes a person outside the fold of Islam.

No, there's nothing wrong with placating your husband in something that doesn't cause you harm or require you to fall into *haraam* (e.g., If your husband believes that the hijab of a woman must be a certain specific color, then it's no problem to wear that color, even if you disagree with his Islamic view on the matter). However, placating a man is not the same as changing your entire religious point of view to follow his, and it's not the same as being required to subject yourself to harm or to obey him over Allah.

In fact, if a Muslim man is married to a Jewish or Christian woman, he isn't allowed to compel her to convert to Islam. This is because the sacredness of the soul in Islam is so central to our faith that even when a person's religious point of view is fundamentally incorrect (in the Islamic lens), they are free to follow it undisturbed, as there is no compulsion in religion, as mentioned in the Qur'an:

لَآ إِكْرَاهَ فِى ٱلدِّينِ قَد تَّبَيَّنَ ٱلرُّشْدُ مِنَ ٱلْغَيِّ فَمَن يَكْفُرْ بِٱلطَّٰغُوتِ وَيُؤْمِنۢ بِٱللَّهِ فَقَدِ ٱسْتَمْسَكَ بِٱلْعُرْوَةِ ٱلْوُثْقَىٰ لَا ٱنفِصَامَ لَهَا وَٱللَّهُ سَمِيعٌ عَلِيمٌ ﴿٢٥٦﴾

"There shall be no compulsion in [acceptance of] the religion. The right course has become clear from the wrong. So whoever disbelieves in Taghut (false gods and evil leaders calling to *shirk*) and believes in Allah has grasped the most trustworthy handhold with no break in it. And Allah is Hearing and Knowing."
—*Al-Baqarah* (2:256)

This is what is meant by the Islamic model of religion being soul-centered. In divine supremacy, **the sacredness of the human soul is so paramount to our faith that we are *obligated* to respect the spiritual boundaries of other people's faith.** Therefore, even non-Muslims are granted religious freedom of choice, even when we genuinely believe (or know) their faith practice to be fundamentally incorrect.

Yes, we can (and should) *invite* non-Muslims to the right path. But we cannot force them to accept this invitation. (In fact, the very meaning of the Arabic term *da'wah* is literally "invitation"). This is because in Islam, each person's soul and relationship with their Creator is their own domain, not anyone else's—even if that person is their spouse. How that person treats their soul (or their spouse) is subjected to Allah's final interrogation and judgment in the Hereafter, not ours in this world.

If this is the case for respecting the spiritual boundaries of a disbeliever who is quite obviously on the wrong path, then how much more so is this the case when respecting the spiritual boundaries of a believing woman—a person who is already worshipping Allah properly and has already accepted the correct path of Islam?

Fourteen

It's About Superiority and Entitlement, Not Leadership or Protection

In male supremacy, as alluded to earlier, the divinely assigned role of men as the leaders in the home and society (i.e., *qawwaamah*) is viewed as indicative of a core life purpose rooted in a "male superiority" birthright. This, instead of viewing *qawwaamah* as a heavy divine assignment rooted in a weighty *amaanah* (trust and responsibility) for which men will be called to account on the Day of Judgment—and for which the dereliction or abuse of it will subject many men to severe punishment in the Hellfire.

In the Islamic model of religion, *qawwaamah* incites in a sincere man of taqwaa heart-trembling fear of Allah, as well as an elevated mindset that is focused on serving Allah alone in this world. This is a divine assignment that he carries out in a space of humility and divine reverence so that his imperfect, sinfully inclined soul will be safe from Allah's torment in the Hereafter. As such, when he fulfills his obligation of protecting Allah's female servants and keeping them safe from harm, he does it in a place of humbleness and gratitude for the immeasurable blessing of being divinely gifted with a feminine presence in his life.

When the Western model of religion is introduced into Islam, the meanings of spiritual concepts already clarified by Allah and His Messenger ﷺ change into something entirely different from what was intended at the time of revelation. This is because a person whose nafs is addicted to *dhulm* (wrongdoing, abuse, or oppression) lives with a spiritual sickness of the heart, inciting him to eagerly follow the darkness of Shaytaan's misguidance over the spiritual light of Allah's right guidance. As a result, this person of *dhulm* (i.e., wrongdoer) creates religious dissension on earth.

In the Qur'an, Allah says:

وَمَآ أَرْسَلْنَا مِن قَبْلِكَ مِن رَّسُولٍ وَلَا نَبِيٍّ إِلَّآ إِذَا تَمَنَّىٰٓ أَلْقَى الشَّيْطَٰنُ فِىٓ أُمْنِيَّتِهِۦ فَيَنسَخُ ٱللَّهُ مَا يُلْقِى ٱلشَّيْطَٰنُ ثُمَّ يُحْكِمُ ٱللَّهُ ءَايَٰتِهِۦ ۗ وَٱللَّهُ عَلِيمٌ حَكِيمٌ ﴿٥٢﴾ لِّيَجْعَلَ مَا يُلْقِى ٱلشَّيْطَٰنُ فِتْنَةً لِّلَّذِينَ فِى قُلُوبِهِم مَّرَضٌ وَٱلْقَاسِيَةِ قُلُوبُهُمْ ۗ وَإِنَّ ٱلظَّٰلِمِينَ لَفِى شِقَاقٍ بَعِيدٍ ﴿٥٣﴾

"And We did not send before you any messenger or prophet except that when he spoke [or recited], Shaytaan (Satan) threw into it [some misunderstanding]. But Allah abolishes that which Shaytaan throws in; then Allah makes precise His *ayaat*. And Allah is Knowing and Wise. [That is] so He may make what Shaytaan throws in a trial for those within whose hearts is disease and those hard of heart. And indeed, the wrongdoers are in extreme dissension."
—Al-Hajj (22:52-53)

This is why in Islamicized male supremacy, the Qur'anic concept of *qawwaamah* (divinely assigned male leadership and protection of women) incites in misguided Muslim men a feeling of *kibr* (spiritually damaging pride), narcissistic self-importance, and a superiority complex. This is also why they can easily quote from the Qur'an to bolster their *kibr* and increase their *dhulm* instead of seeking through the Qur'an a source of healing for their spiritual diseases of the heart and mercy from Allah for their shortcomings. As a result, they do not experience the soul-nourishing guidance and mercy from Allah's revelation that a man (or woman) of taqwaa does. Instead, they experience only spiritual loss and self-deception.

In the Qur'an, Allah says:

وَنُنَزِّلُ مِنَ ٱلْقُرْءَانِ مَا هُوَ شِفَآءٌ وَرَحْمَةٌ لِّلْمُؤْمِنِينَ وَلَا يَزِيدُ
ٱلظَّٰلِمِينَ إِلَّا خَسَارًا ﴿٨٢﴾

"And We send down of the Qur'an that which is a healing and mercy for the believers, but it does not increase the wrongdoers except in loss."
—*Al-Israa'* (17:82)

For male supremacists, the Qur'anic guidance intended to offer believing men spiritual gain is merely an opportunity for them to run after every opportunity for spiritual loss. This is because in this world, **their goal is self-satisfaction and the fulfillment of their desires** (e.g., ego-boosting, feeling superior to women, using women as conduits of their masculinity, etc.). Therefore, they arrogantly turn down almost every divine invitation for healing their spiritual and emotional wounds (especially if it comes from a woman reminding them to fear Allah). They also turn down almost every divine invitation to seek Allah's mercy as a way to purify their nafs from the darkness of sin and dhulm they are drowning in.

They Treat Reminders with Arrogance and Mockery

In fact, many male supremacists treat any reminder to fear Allah, especially if it comes from a woman, as a moment to arrogantly discredit the woman by mentioning religious texts that (allegedly) suggest that men are unilaterally superior to women and that women are evil creatures who will fill the Hellfire. As a result, they run the risk of throwing their own selves headlong into Hellfire by dedicating themselves to a sin of the heart that even a grain of it will prevent them from entering into Paradise.

Prophet Muhammad (peace be upon him) said, "No one who has an atom's weight of *kibr* (pride) in his heart will enter Paradise." A man said, "O Messenger of Allah, what if a man likes his clothes and his shoes to look good?" He said, "Allah is Beautiful and loves beauty. **Kibr means rejecting the truth and looking down on people**" (Sahih Muslim).

And male supremacists are clinging on to both meanings of kibr: rejecting the truth of Islam's divine supremacy (and preferring instead the West's male supremacy) while looking down on Allah's female servants as if it is a divine right.

Tragically, if they continue on this path of spiritual loss and seeking self-importance more than humility, they run the risk of having no spiritual resources at the time of death, when their soul is about to be extracted from their bodies and when Shaytaan is amping up his invitations to misguidance, much of which they already accepted before this moment.

Those who accept that final invitation to the Hellfire will do so because they didn't nurture enough emaan and taqwaa (i.e., protecting their soul from harm) in this world when they had a chance. (May Allah protect us). Yet, previously, these were people who went about the earth in self-importance, arrogantly seeing other people as evil and inferior while imagining themselves to be spiritually pure and superior.

These are people Allah grants the added humiliation of entering Hellfire only to find that the people they counted as evil are not there alongside them, as these so-called inferior "evil ones" are in Paradise instead. This will be a moment of such shocking disbelief to the person who was so full of certainty and arrogance in this world when labeling *others* as evil and inferior. In fact, this humiliated person will be so shocked that he doesn't see these evil, inferior people being punished in the Hellfire that he will quite literally question if his eyes are deceiving him.

In the Qur'an, Allah says:

وَقَالُوا۟ مَا لَنَا لَا نَرَىٰ رِجَالًا كُنَّا نَعُدُّهُم مِّنَ ٱلْأَشْرَارِ ﴿٦٢﴾
أَتَّخَذْنَٰهُمْ سِخْرِيًّا أَمْ زَاغَتْ عَنْهُمُ ٱلْأَبْصَٰرُ ﴿٦٣﴾

"And they will say, 'What is the matter with us that we see not men (i.e., people) whom we used to count among the bad ones? Did we take them as an object of mockery, or have [our] eyes failed to perceive them?"
—*Saad* (38:62-63)

Fifteen

Men Are Superior to Women in Everything?

Here, it is relevant to highlight another side of the dark psychology of male supremacy, wherein *qawwaamah* is seen as a birthright of "male superiority" more than a weighty divine assignment of a heavy responsibility and severe accountability. This gives us a deeper understanding of just how far the lizard's hole of male supremacy goes in the misguided Muslim's mind:

In the male-centered Western model of religion, a man's "superiority" is viewed as both unilateral and limitless. As such, it is viewed as reaching all areas of superiority in life (e.g., wealth, intelligence, strength, piety, religious knowledge, worldly success, etc.) without exception.

This is especially the case when male supremacist men compare their (alleged) unlimited superior entitlement to the (alleged) unlimited inferior subjugation they feel women are obligated to accept in this world. Therefore, as it relates to any "superior" accomplishments that Allah has granted women in their earthly experience, male supremacist men see their own "male superiority" as a zero-sum game.

In other words, in the mind of a male supremacist man (or woman), any worldly accomplishment that a woman has been granted automatically subtracts from a man's worldly accomplishment. Thus, any worldly "superiority" that a woman enjoys in this world means that it was wrongly taken from a man or that it was wrongly given to a woman when it *should have* been given to a man. (This is why male supremacists are ultimately angry with Allah more than they are angry with women, something I discuss in brief later).

This is similar to how white supremacists view the worldly success of people of color. Worldly superiority belongs exclusively to them, so people of color are seen as "stealing" from them if they have any superior worldly success (or access) that a random white person doesn't have (even without the same level of intelligence, talent, and skill as the person of color).

Additionally, male supremacists *also* believe that by the mere fact that a woman is successful in a "superior" worldly matter (even if it's outside of her control, like divinely gifted intelligence), she is doing something sinful or unrighteous, "untraditional" or is being un-womanly (or "un-feminine"). This is because male supremacists view worldly success as a male-only (or masculine) domain or as a "male superiority" birthright. Therefore, a woman's worldly accomplishments are viewed as inherently sinful or impious, or as improper or "unbecoming" of a "real woman."

This is because beneath the surface of the superiority complex of a male supremacist is a thinly veiled *inferiority complex*, as is the case with narcissism. This deeply buried feeling of low worth makes the male supremacist obsessed with ensuring that the male is granted worldly favor above the female in literally *everything*.

This is why male supremacists openly *claim* to view women as inherently "less than" human beings (while in truth, deep inside, they feel helpless and worthless without a woman in their life). This is also why men influenced by male supremacist cults like Red Pill feel so angered and threatened by intelligent, successful, and wealthy women.

Male supremacists intuitively know that things like intelligence, success, and wealth are "superior" worldly traits, so they feel these divine favors should be granted exclusively to men. This is also why men influenced by male supremacist ideology feel emasculated if their wife makes more money than they do. It's also why they feel intimidated by "educated women," or if a woman has more Islamic knowledge than they do.

But they *claim* they don't like these things in a woman because it makes a woman unfeminine. But the truth is, the very sight of a woman's divinely gifted greatness—and her obvious worldly superiority over a man in wealth, success, intelligence, and religion—makes *him* feel unmanly.

They Project Worthlessness onto Women

To fight their own self-perception of worthlessness within themselves, male supremacist men project onto successful women their own internalized feelings of "low value" (e.g., *"What does she need me for then?"*) by calling successful, self-loving, intelligent women what they feel about themselves: low value.

When these men choose to actively seek out successful, intelligent women in a relationship, it is most often for the sole purpose of spiritually or emotionally abusing her, shaming her into shrinking and self-erasure, and doing everything in their power to make her feel small. Why? Because until he chooses to heal and access manhood from within, this is a self-emasculated man's only access to feeling big and powerful and self-important in this world.

The more that an unhealed, self-emasculated man can witness the restless servitude and exhaustive self-sacrifice of a woman who is gifted with superior worldly favors that he doesn't have, the more he can access the *feelings* of manhood. These are manly feelings that he desperately desires but feels utterly incapable of accessing on his own, as he feels utterly worthless without a female conduit.

The High-Value Girl-Child Wife

These unhealed, self-emasculated men's feelings of low worth are also why they obsess over marrying young girls whose age is closer to childhood than adulthood. They feel like they need by their side a wife with little to no life experience or knowledge of self. This allows them to *also* show up with little to no self-knowledge of manhood or with little to no meaningful experience with true masculinity. In other words, they want to be evenly yoked.

Deep down, they know that their fragile egos cannot handle the slightest challenge to show up as a real man of taqwaa in truth. Consequently, they require a woman who brings absolutely *nothing* to the table except an empty mind, an attractive body, and robot-like submission. Their spiritual weakness, emotional fragility, and wounded masculinity literally cannot handle anything else.

This is why a woman's natural ageing process scares them so much. They know that an experienced woman will come with real-life feminine maturity (which means real-life manly accountability for the man), and that isn't valuable to them. Why? Because they haven't invested in real-life manly maturity themselves.

So, these men are absolutely speaking the truth when they call mature women "low value." However, what they don't tell you is this: This label is merely a projection of where they themselves are in life at that time. It's not a statement of the actual value this woman holds in truth.

Moreover, no man with an ounce of taqwaa, self-respect, or true manhood as defined by Allah would speak about Allah's female servants in this—even if these are women he would never prefer for marriage for himself.

They Want Her Caged and Frozen in Time

Male supremacist, emotionally underdeveloped men, feel they need an emotionally underdeveloped wife. But the challenge is finding ways to keep her that way. After all, gaining emotional maturity, self-awareness, and personal wisdom is a natural, healthy part of life on earth.

But in male supremacy, the natural ageing and maturing process is unacceptable for a "good woman" to experience, as they see it as lowering a woman's value and compromising her piety. (Of course, in divine supremacy, the truth is the exact opposite, which is why our mother Khadijah remained the most beloved and highly valued wife to our Prophet ﷺ until his death).

This obsession with possessing as a wife a "forever-caged, girl-child frozen in time" is where spiritual abuse and weaponizing male-supremacist interpretations of religion come in handy. And these men actively do their homework. So, they use selective righteousness in finding ways to keep women small while subsequently blaming it on God and religion. Then they share notes.

This is why, as a general rule, male supremacist men oppose a woman getting an education, starting a business (even if it's from home), having her own money, or even gaining "too much" Islamic knowledge. They are actually petrified of their wife having a life outside of them. Why? Because deep down, they fear that if she gets even a whiff of life outside their man-child cage built for husband-worship, she will run for the hills.

So, the male supremacist man invents more and more ways to keep his "girl-child" wife imprisoned at home and mentally frozen in time as a "forever child" in a woman's body. Thus, they find ways to keep updating their wife's mental and religious programming, which tells her that she has no meaningful purpose in life except to offer her husband good food, good sex, and quiet submission.

But meanwhile, the husband remains anxiously unsettled, as all he can think about is, *If only I can find a way to keep her away from the feminists* (a word he uses to describe every woman who has enough self-love, life experience, and Islamic knowledge to know that Allah would never require His female servants to live like this, whether married or not).

Sixteen

Men of Taqwaa Love and Appreciate Women

S o many of us are taught our faith in ways that tell us that someone else is responsible for our lives and souls, or that we have rights over other people's lives and souls in ways that the Creator did not grant us. Or we are taught that we have rights over other people's lives and souls in ways that only the Creator has over His creation.

This phenomenon has caused false piety to become so widespread during these Last Days that most of us genuinely have no idea what taqwaa-centered femininity or taqwaa-centered masculinity even looks like. And due to the worldly perks that so many of us receive while living in false piety, many of us don't even *want* to know what true femininity or true masculinity looks like from a space of taqwaa.

What Is Taqwaa and Why Is it Important?

In Islamic spirituality, *taqwaa* is first and foremost rooted in protecting our souls from harm. Then from this space of spiritual self-protection, taqwaa inspires us to remain mindful, fearful, and trusting of Allah in ways that nourish our souls, better our lives, and inspire within us self-discipline, self-accountability, and compassionate presence (with ourselves and others).

Taqwaa Inspires Love and Appreciation of Women

For men in particular, taqwaa inspires them to humbly and sincerely uphold the Sunnah of compassionate masculinity. As such, if they view their divine assignment through the lens of any notions of "superiority," it is through striving to uphold the traits of the truly superior man (i.e., the best of men as described in the prophetic narrations). For example:

Abu Huraira (may Allah be pleased with him) reported that the Messenger of Allah ﷺ said, "The most complete of believers in faith are those with the best character, and **the best of you are the best in behavior to their women**" (Sunan al-Tirmidhī 1162, Sahih by Al-Tirmidhi).

Aisha (may Allah be pleased with her) reported that the Messenger of Allah ﷺ said, "**The best of you are the best to their families**, and I am the best to my family…" (Source: Sunan al-Tirmidhī 3895, Sahih by Al-Albaani).

Abu Huraira (may Allah be pleased with him) reported that the Messenger of Allah ﷺ said, "**A believing man should not hate a believing woman.** If he dislikes one of her characteristics, he will be pleased with another" Sahih Muslim 1468b).

Abdullah ibn Amr (may Allah be pleased with him) reported that the Messenger of Allah ﷺ said, "The world is enjoyment and **the best enjoyment in the world is a pious woman**" (Ṣaḥīḥ Muslim 1467).

Historically, believing men have also expressed their appreciation for the immense blessings that women bring to their lives. For example, the famous scholar Ibn al-Qayyim (may Allah have mercy on him) said: "**Women are the cause of happiness of the heart.** That's why they're also called the reason for happiness of the soul" (*Rawdat al-Muhibeen*).

Ibn al-Qayyim also said, "Women are one half of society, which gives birth to the other half. So, it is as if they are the entire society."

Also, the author, Dr.Hesham Al-Awadi, said: 'If you were to omit women from Islamic history, there would be no Islamic history" (*Women Inspired By the Beloved*).

PART FOUR

Truth Sets Us Free

Truths About Male Supremacy

"If a man does not process and integrate his anger, or find a healthy release for it, it is his relationship, his loved ones that will suffer from it. Many men are deeply angry. Angry at themselves for sabotaging their life and their relationships, angry at their father who didn't embody healthy masculine energy, or angry at the world.

Anger in itself is not the problem, the problem is how we use it, what we do with it. Anger, if harnessed in the right way, can allow a man to strengthen his leadership, to lead the world into a safer and better place. Anger can strengthen his connection to his archaic protective instincts, to protect his loved ones, to shield them from the negativity and pain of the world, and his own shadow.

Anger can turn into his power, yet in order for this to happen, he needs to connect with his anger, and use it to break through his limiting beliefs, his wounds, until his anger turns into loving service to the world."

—Lorin Krenn, author of *Understand Women Better*

Seventeen

Male Supremacy Harms Men

Men are suffering too. Tragically, the suicide rate amongst men is significantly high. Some studies estimate that men account for 75 to 80% of deaths by suicide. In the USA alone, the suicide rate amongst men is reported to be four times that of women (HeadsUpGuys.org, 2023).

Amongst the reasons researchers and mental health experts give for these staggering suicide rates is that men have been indoctrinated with destructive ideas of "manhood."

As a general rule, boys are socialized to disconnect from the most vulnerable parts of themselves in efforts to always be "strong" and to avoid appearing "weak." Consequently, men are far less likely than women to admit when they need help mentally or emotionally, let alone seek it out or openly ask for it.

From childhood through adulthood, boys and men are routinely socialized to always be in control—of themselves and others. So, when they feel utterly helpless and find their inner world collapsing in ways that they can't quite make sense of, they have little to no emotional tools to weather the storm. They are also unable to find ways to still feel "manly" while experiencing this loss of control.

For Muslims living upon the soul-centered Islamic model of religion (i.e., divine supremacy), we might notice right away that these harmful definitions of manhood contradict true masculinity. This is because they are in sharp contrast to the lived experience of Prophet Muhammad (peace be upon him).

From the very beginning of revelation, the Messenger of Allah ﷺ was deeply in touch with his own emotional vulnerability and human limitations. As such, when he received revelation for the first time and felt overwhelmed with confusion and self-doubt, he immediately sought help and refuge in his beloved wife Khadijah (may Allah be pleased with her). Moreover, the Prophet ﷺ even followed his wife's advice about seeking out the perspective of her cousin Waraqah in Nawfal (may Allah be pleased with him) about this confusing experience.

Even beyond this incident and throughout his entire life, the Prophet ﷺ was well-known for seeking out the advice and counsel of his wives, as well as that of the Companions, whenever he needed others' input or whenever he desired a fresh perspective.

Human Greatness Is in Humility

Unfortunately, systems of harm and dhulm like male supremacy require men to disconnect from the deepest, most human parts of themselves. This is why they are obsessed with "male superiority" and texts that make them feel more "god-like" than human (e.g., a woman prostrating to her husband).

It's also why they obsessively share these things in contexts that call for safe masculine presence more than claims of male superiority. Insecure, unhealed men need to feel superior at all times, so they are utterly incapable of sitting with the slightest discomfort incited by self-awareness or self-accountability, especially in the presence of the feminine who is hurting or healing.

In contrast, healed men of taqwaa, who are secure in their manhood, embrace humility as a way of life. Any superiority that exists in them becomes obvious with their strength of character, compassionate presence, and principled integrity. They never need to say the quiet part out loud. Their very presence and actions speak for themselves. It is only men living in insecure masculinity who feel the need to *claim* superiority out loud. This is because their lives are often proclaiming something entirely different behind the scenes..

Insecure, unhealed men feel like it is an assault on their manhood to show any "inferior" human traits like weakness, especially in front of women. This is because women are the one group they can always feel superior to, no matter how badly things are going in their own lives. In this, they are like the poverty-stricken, pathologically insecure racist who sees his only hope for a semblance of human dignity in telling himself, "Well, at least I'm better than a nigger." So, male supremacist men go around telling themselves and any woman in earshot (or who they hope will read their trolling comments online), "Well, at least I'm better than women."

However, they don't realize that the human greatness they are desperately seeking can never be found on this path. This path of constantly proclaiming self-importance can, however, wreak havoc on their mental health, throw their personal lives and finances into disarray, and sabotage any chance of a healthy romantic relationship long before it even begins.

Eighteen

The Lie They Tell Us About Men

Some time ago, I was reflecting on something deeply troubling that I keep hearing Muslim men and women repeat as "absolute truth" about men, love, and relationships. *But why do they keep saying this?* I thought to myself, *because it's absolutely __not__ true.*

As I went through my own journey of love and solitude, I've reflected on this oft-repeated lie and pondered the likely motivations behind it. But for now, let's look at the lie itself, as it's a lie that even many "relationship coaches" are participating in spreading about men and marriage:

LIE	Men don't care about women's talents, intelligence, or worldly accomplishments.
TRUTH	While men generally don't care about these things in the same *way* that women care about men's, men absolutely do care about these things.

And the proofs for this are numerous, not only in worldly research, human experience, and common sense, but also in our Islamic faith itself.

Let's start with some divine truths (which I cover in this chapter) and then at some worldly truths (which I cover in the two chapters that follow this one).

Divine Truths that Dispel the Lie

Reflect on the talents, intelligence, and success of our Mother Khadijah (may Allah be pleased with her).

What Muslim with even a grain of emaan (sincere faith) in his heart would boldly claim that our beloved Prophet ﷺ cared *nothing* about her divinely gifted worldly talents, accomplishments, and success? That he cared nothing of her worldly status outside of what she offered him in domestic servitude and carnal pleasure in marriage?

Reflect also on the hadith about the seven people under the Shade of Allah on the Day of Judgment. Now, recall the single distinguishing trait of the woman whom a man finds it most challenging to resist temptation from. She is a woman with a unique combination of both beauty <u>and</u> worldly status.

If a woman's worldly status meant nothing to men, it would have been sufficient for Allah to inspire His Prophet and Messenger ﷺ to mention only a woman's remarkable beauty in inciting temptation. However, **Allah knows the hearts of His servants (male and female) better than we know (or admit) ourselves,** and so He knows very well the hearts of the men He created.

And in the heart of nearly every man, a woman's worldly status raises her desirability and attractiveness manifold in his eyes. This is so much so that there is a special reward for the man of taqwaa (God-consciousness and self-discipline) who chooses his soul over caving into temptation by a woman of remarkable beauty and distinct worldly status.

How They Defend the Lie

"But a woman's worldly status means nothing to a man when he's in the privacy of his home and wants her respect, submissiveness, and intimacy!" they say.

Yes, but that's true for <u>all</u> human beings, including women in their feelings toward men.

As a woman, if I'm seeking emotional safety, compassion, and connection with my husband, what do I care about his worldly status, accomplishments, or even wealth at that moment? Like nearly all women, at that time, what I value most is connecting with my husband's heart and soul. I'm not thinking about his accolades, intelligence, or net worth (or whether he fits into some elusive category of a "high value man").

In fact, every single day, women walk away from wealthy, accomplished, "high value men" and never look back. Similarly, every single day, men walk away from beautiful, submissive "traditional" women.

These are often women who gave up everything to be with these men. These women often bypassed every personal opportunity for their own worldly success, status, and wealth, imagining that this sacrifice would make them highly valued and deeply cherished by their husbands. These women were ready, eager, and willing to dedicate the rest of their lives to this "happily ever after" marriage and to being *only* wives and mothers until they died.

Yet still, their men left them (or gave these women no reasonable option except to walk away themselves).

Nineteen

But When a Man Loves a Woman...

O n the other hand, every single day, talented, accomplished, successful women of high worldly status are deeply loved, cherished, and *fully taken care of* by their husbands. These are men who appreciate and value every single divinely gifted quality in the woman God blessed them with in marriage.

And amongst these men are those who would never claim that his beloved wife's talents, intelligence, or worldly accomplishments mean nothing to him. This is because these men have the natural, healthy trait of soul-nourishing masculinity that mirrors that of the Prophet ﷺ.

So, when it comes to any woman they love (whether wife, daughter, sister, etc.), the truth of a healthy man's heart is this: **What hurts her hurts him, and what brings her joy brings him joy.**

Therefore, if a woman's talents, hobbies, and worldly accomplishments matter to her, then they matter to him, and they also bring *him* joy. If for no other reason than seeing her happy makes him happy.

This basic truth about men is not even including the multitudes of men in this world who also appreciate a woman's worldly status, talents, and accomplishments because of the immeasurable benefit this woman brings to the world with these gifts, even if the man himself has no personal connection to this highly accomplished woman in real life.

Twenty

Their Phobias and Phantoms

S o, why then are so many of us committed to the lie that tells us that men don't care about a woman's talents, intelligence, or worldly accomplishments, while in fact the exact opposite is true?

The answer is more complicated than any one person can break down effectively. But I can say this: **It has a lot to do with male supremacist ideology and their phobia of and hatred for anything that gives women leverage in this world.** This is especially the case when that worldly leverage makes women feel good about themselves outside the context of centering a man (even if she is, in fact, in a relationship with a man), or that inspires women to feel content and fulfilled outside a relationship with a man, especially if she has no desire to ever get married (or remarried).

Their Phobia of Women's Joy

This phobia of women's worldly leverage is why male supremacists call nearly *everything* "feminism" if it benefits a woman's life in any way, or even if it merely bolsters her self-esteem or inspires within her healthy self-love in things that she does for herself that aren't male-centered.

It's also why, amongst Muslim male supremacists, they view it as practically a religious obligation to apply *soo'u dhann* (the worst possible assumption and interpretation) to anything a woman does that isn't focused on stroking the male ego. They genuinely believe it's sinful for a woman to enjoy life outside the context of centering them. This is why, for many of them, **even a woman's relationship with Allah threatens their manhood** (which in their mind is equivalent to falling into sin based on their male supremacist religion), hence the imam-therapist's point of view mentioned at the beginning of this book.

They Create Phantoms to Fight

When it comes to male supremacists' concocted, knee-jerk definitions of *feminist*, it's helpful to understand that their interpretations of feminism are completely unrelated to what the word *feminist* actually means. It's also completely unrelated to what this word means to the women who identify with the term. This is why they apply it willy-nilly, even to women who neither use the term in reality nor fit the definition of it in truth.

To understand this puzzling phenomenon, you need to understand only this: **Feminism is a phantom enemy that male supremacists have created in their minds.** It allows them to feel manly on a phantom battlefield.

This isn't to say that feminism itself doesn't exist, or even that *some* iterations of it aren't problematic. It's merely to say that in *their* use of the term, male supremacists view "feminism" in a way that doesn't exist in reality. Instead, **their definition of feminism is based on a make-believe world that they've created to feel like men.** Why? Because they're too terrified to live in the reality of the personal and collective lack of manhood they live in, in truth. Moreover, they are too petrified to face their own inner darknesses of the nafs, which are rooted in cowardly, self-emasculation that they chose (and cultivated) all on their own.

So, they choose a make-believe world and a phantom enemy to fight. Now, keep in mind, **it's no accident that their biggest enemy in even their *phantom* world is the very group of people (i.e., women) whom they claim to be the weakest, most inferior, and incapable** of Allah's creation.

Here is where they are telling on themselves. How so? Because in their own weak, emasculated states, it is only a weak, inferior enemy whom they feel powerful enough to fight and continuously triumph over. This is because even in their *imaginations*, they wouldn't dare enter a <u>real</u> battle, where they would be required to show up as real men.

Their World of Make-Believe Strength

In their world of make-believe, male supremacists are strong, powerful Marvel-like men. They are courageous "soldiers" fighting against agents of darkness who are destroying the world.

As alluded to above, they create these phantom enemies and phantom battlefields because a world of make-believe is the only place they feel safe. It's the only place they feel courageous and strong. It's the only place can fight real enemies and real darkness while stopping real destruction in the world.

But really, they are only fighting themselves.

How so? It's the infamous psychology of "punching down," which is a tactic used by school bullies and other "courageous cowards" worldwide. These are people who outwardly show unapologetic bravado in fights and can be seen eagerly stepping into proverbial boxing rings all the time. But you'll notice that opposite them on the ropes is never their equal, as they wouldn't dare pick a fight with someone in their own weight division.

What Does Feminism Mean to Them, Exactly?

As aforementioned, male supremacists call nearly *everything* "feminism" if it benefits a woman's life in any way. They apply this label to even things that merely bolster a woman's self-esteem. They also apply it to any evidence of a woman's self-love.

In male-supremacist speak, as a general rule, the only actual, non-make-believe reality that needs to be present to justify applying the label feminist to a woman is this: ***Is a man being centered in a way that makes her insignificant and small?* If the answer is no, then she's a feminist.**

It really is that dimwitted and simple-minded. But that's how crippling insecurity and low self-worth works, especially in the mind of a weak man masquerading as a "strong" truth-teller.

To get a better idea of how this works, here are some examples of where the label feminist would likely be applied and will almost always carry a negative, derogatory, "evil" meaning in the mind of a male supremacist:

- *I came across a woman who made me self-reflect. She must be a feminist!*
- *I came across a woman who disagreed with me. She must be a feminist!*
- *I came across a woman who's divorced and isn't seeking remarriage. She must be a feminist!*
- *I came across a woman who has more knowledge than me (or other men). She must be a feminist!*
- *I came across a woman who's out of my league. She must be a feminist!*

- *I came across a woman who doesn't worship men. She is most definitely a feminist!*
- *I came across a woman who is telling men to fear Allah. She's not only a feminist, but she's also a misandrist!*
- *I came across a woman who was abused by men and is now helping other women heal. She's a feminist, a misandrist, and an enemy of Islam!*

The Feminist Label Is an Ego-Protector

Interestingly, male supremacists treat the word *feminist* in the male-centered way that they treat everything in their religion of male supremacy: They make it all about them.

So, if they're feeling triggered or angered by a woman, she's a feminist. If they feel intimidated by a woman's knowledge or intelligence, she's a feminist. If they feel emasculated because they fear they'll likely never enjoy the level of world success or wealth that a woman is enjoying, she's a feminist. If they see a woman worshipping Allah and loving herself and her faith outside the context of marriage, she's a feminist. On and on and on…

In other words, in the world of male supremacy, the label feminist has absolutely nothing to do with a woman's reality. Rather, it has everything to do with a man's, most especially his inner world.

For this reason, when he feels the slightest sensation of an inner loss of control, the male supremacist man rushes to call the object of his fury (or unattainable desire) a feminist. This is his way of discrediting and diminishing the power and significance of an "out of his league" woman. He also hopes through this ad hominem attack that he'll discredit and vilify this woman in the eyes of other people. This is how he protects his hurt ego and how he battles his own feelings of powerlessness.

But most of all, with this personal attack and knee-jerk feminist label, **the male supremacist hopes to discredit and vilify this woman in front of herself.** In this, he hopes to diminish her self-esteem, to make her doubt herself, and to humiliate her into retreating into a space of crippling shame and insecurity. This is because this is the inner world he himself lives in each day.

Twenty-one
Their Bait and Switch

W e've already established that in the mental world of the male supremacist, the label *feminist* rarely (if ever) is about conveying truth, whether that truth is about the woman herself or about the word itself. Rather, **applying the label feminist is about restoring a man's ego after experiencing feelings of loss of control, of powerlessness, and of masculine inferiority**, especially in the presence of a strong, accomplished, worldly "superior" feminine.

This is why male supremacists almost always apply to the word *feminist* the absolutely worst possible meaning. It's also why, in most cases, they do not even *attempt* to add nuance, critical thought, or exception to what they're saying, claiming, or implying. To them, if they feel a woman is a feminist (and here, emphasis is on the word "feel"), then she's a feminist, even if she herself doesn't even identify as one. And the label feminist is almost always equal to "evil."

In this moment, they couldn't care less what the truth is, whether regarding the various definitions of the word *feminist* itself, or regarding what the truth is about this woman (or a Muslim's use of this word) in front of Allah. This is because in male supremacy, the mind, desires, and assumptions of a man always reign supreme, even over the divine.

This is one of many reasons why **male supremacy is the diametrical opposite of divine supremacy.** The divine only matters when they can invoke Him to claim superiority over women. After that, the actual nuanced truth of the religion that they claim to be part of is irrelevant and useless.

"Low Value" Religion and Women

In this way, male supremacists treat religion how they treat women. When it's serving them and their desires, it's "high value." When it's not, it's "low value." Or it is completely useless.

Make no mistake. Muslim male supremacists are not here to serve Islam. They are here to manipulate Islam as a tool to serve themselves.

This is why, as aforementioned, they have no qualms about calling a Muslim woman a feminist when she doesn't even identify as one herself. Meanwhile, in the same breath, they'll *also* claim that the word *feminist* has only evil, anti-Islamic meanings. In other words, they have no problem whatsoever *rushing* to slander a female servant of Allah, and with this, implying that she is an evil, enemy of Islam. Why? Because she happened to irk them (even if unintentionally) or because her presence or intelligence alone triggered their insecurities.

This is also why they have no qualms about vilifying a Muslim woman who *does* identify as a feminist but has made it undeniably clear that she defines it in a way that aligns with Islamic principles, regardless of how some non-Muslim feminists define the term. Yet still, even this woman is considered an evil, enemy of Islam. Why? Well, because how dare a woman use a label that makes them feel less of a man.

The Only Time Feminism Is Good

In the world of male supremacy, the word feminist almost always carries a negative, derogatory, evil meaning. However, **there's one notable exception to this general rule**, especially for Muslim men who are male supremacists but happen to be involved in public-facing *daw'ah* efforts, where they speak at interfaith events, inviting others to Islam.

Now, keep in mind these events are often attended by an audience that includes beautiful, physically attractive non-Muslim women. This is where these anti-feminist men suddenly find nuance, balance, and even a bit of self-honesty about how *some* definitions of feminism and *some* iterations of the feminist movement are not only good, positive, and praiseworthy but are also *Islamic* in their meanings and goals.

So, as a strategy aimed at earning new converts to Islam, these male supremacist men somehow have the presence of mind to invoke feminism in its *true* meaning of the term, at least as it's defined by the women sitting in front of them. Why? There are at least three key reasons for this:

1) **It's a religious marketing strategy.** Here, the aim is to gain as many converts to Islam as possible, so the "da'wah bro" is heavily incentivized to tell the female audience the truth. Intuitively, these men know that the women sitting in front of them are most likely sincere, goodhearted people. They know these women only want to be treated well, to be respected as full human beings, and to build a respectable life for themselves. These women also want to live their lives free from harm and obsessive control. They also likely desire their own wealth, career, or business. And they have no desire to be forced into an unwanted marriage or stuck in an abusive one. These are quite literally the *only things* these women are often seeking

through the feminist movement—and incidentally, these very things are also rights and options that Islam grants to women. So, the da'wah bro tells them the truth.

2) **It's an ego boost and power move.** In other words, in this context, the da'wah bro's honesty about the intersection between women's rights in Islam and *some* iterations of feminism is an ego boost and a power move. It's his artful way of navigating (and respecting) the relevant power dynamics at play. For example, in the United States, at an event like this, the power dynamics are in favor of white supremacy. And of course, the power of white supremacy trumps the power of non-white *male* supremacy, no matter how much this man *claims* to be superior to all women. So, he speaks the language of white feminism because that's his target audience. It's also his only hope of having leverage or being taken seriously in this situation. It also gives him the power to steer the conversation in a way that keeps it on his terms while his audience is captivated.

3) **It's a "bait and switch" trap.** Most significantly, as it relates to male supremacy, his truth-telling in this case is part of a "bait and switch" religious marketing scheme. This is a strategy often used by hunters and predators as a means of capturing their prey. Here, the target prey are "potential wives" or potential female converts. So, if any of these beautiful women feel impressed by what they heard, they'll eagerly sign up for Islam, thinking they'll be even more honored and respected in a faith that so obviously upholds women's rights. But once they become Muslim or marry any of these men, they find themselves treated as useless property. Then any mention of feminism is

used as evidence of their "Western evil," their lack of Islamic righteousness, their "low value" as wives, and their status as "enemies of Islam" (according to the religion of male supremacy).

In other words, the religious truths of divine supremacy are used to "win the girl," and the dark truths of male supremacy are used to entrap her and keep her.

Twenty-two

Male Supremacists Are Upset with Allah

For male supremacist men, as alluded to earlier, it is literally terrifying (and often enraging) for women to have options outside of them, to experience joy outside of them, and most especially to have fulfillment (or success) in anything that isn't male-centered, or in anything that is deemed "superior" in this world.

This includes worldly talent, remarkable intelligence, or financial success. Why? Because **male supremacists see these "superior" worldly accomplishments as a right belonging exclusively to men.**

Going back to the lie we're often told about men and relationships (i.e., "Men don't care about these things in women!"): It's <u>not</u> a lie propagated by men of taqwaa; it's a lie propagated by male supremacists. But even then, it's still a lie.

It's an Aqeedah Problem with Them

Here's what is true: It is part of the *'aqeedah* (foundational belief system) of male supremacy to view "superior" worldly traits like wealth, success, intelligence, scholarly knowledge, public influence, and high worldly status as masculine-only domains.

This is due to their male-centric religion viewing manhood as indicative of a divinely bestowed "male superior birthright" vs. Islam's divine-centric, soul-centered religion viewing manhood as a divine assignment of responsibility. It isn't a birthright of superiority that is granted to men at birth; it is the unique, *extra tools* to carry out this assignment that is written in their XY-chromosomal assignment at birth.

In other words, in divine supremacy, God has given men everything they need to carry out their manly obligations in this world. It's written in their biology (just as it's written in women's biology to carry out their worldly obligations). Thus, men don't need to use women, feminine servitude, or other external "ego boosts" as conduits of their masculinity. This is what is meant by manhood is an inside job.

Yes, men and women are helpers of each other. But this doesn't mean they're incapable of showing up as full men and women of taqwaa without each other—or even if they happened to marry someone who isn't fulfilling their end of the bargain.

This is why, even amongst the best men (i.e., prophets), you have men like Prophet Noah and Prophet Lot (peace be upon them) who were not only able to show up as real men of taqwaa despite having unrighteous wives, but they were also able to show up as two of the best *of the best* of men.

Similarly, amongst the best of women—i.e., Asiyah, the wife of Pharaoh; Mary, the mother of Jesus; Khadijah, the most beloved wife of the Prophet; and Fatimah, the most beloved daughter of the Prophet (may Allah be pleased with them)—one of them never married, and another was married to an abusive husband. Yet still, they were able to not only fulfill their divine assignment in this world, but they were also able to be written amongst the best women to ever live.

When male supremacist men claim superiority, they often invoke the famous hadith of the Prophet (peace be upon him), where he mentioned how thousands of men reached perfection, but only four women reached perfection.

But here's what they're forgetting: **We're *also* taught that thousands of prophets existed historically**, most of whom we don't know by name, and they were so numerous that we don't even have an exact numerical figure for their precise amount. So, just from a mathematical perspective, this automatically and quite significantly reduces the pool of "superior men," as all the prophets were almost certainly the vast majority of them.

From an Islamic perspective, this makes it highly unlikely that many (or any) of the regular non-prophet men we see walking the world today were included amongst these "superior men" who reached human perfection.

In any case, here's what we do know for sure about all the superior men and women in history: They didn't attain this status by "superior birthright." They attained it by superior integrity, sincerity, and actions. That makes a large part of this equation human choice. But male supremacist men choose to walk around claiming superior rights to things that aren't theirs, even things that Allah Himself has given to many of His female servants.

And *that* is what these men have a problem with: Allah's choices, not women's. But they can't say <u>that</u> quiet part out loud, so they lie.

Why They Lie

As mentioned at the beginning of this chapter, the *'aqeedah* of male supremacy teaches men this: Any and all "superior" worldly accomplishments and sources of success (i.e., divine favors that raise a person's status in this world) are rights belonging exclusively to men. So, they see the idea of men being granted worldly wealth, success, and status as merely evidence of men receiving what is rightly owed to them due to their "male superiority birthright."

This is the reason that male supremacist men are highly incentivized to SAY they don't care about these things in a woman. However, the truth is the exact opposite. They absolutely do care about these things in a woman. They care so much, in fact, that it makes them angry.

In truth, if a man simply doesn't find a particular trait attractive in women, he would simply find a woman who has the traits he likes, then he'd go on with his life. But that's not what male supremacists do. They *obsess* over these traits in women. They make podcasts about these traits in women. They invest time, energy, and money (often that they don't even have, thereby voluntarily going into financial debt) to highlight these traits in women, only to tell the world they don't find these traits attractive. Why? Because the truth is the exact opposite.

These are the very traits they find *most* attractive in this world, so much so that they attach their entire self-worth to possessing these traits. They're just mad that these traits haven't been bestowed on them exclusively.

But here's one thing they *are* telling the truth about on their podcast pics: Male supremacist men often won't choose highly accomplished women as wives. Why? It's not because of a lack of attraction. It's because **they are deeply insecure in their manhood, and they need to feel superior to women at all times.** Therefore, having a wife who is blessed with superiority in *any* category they deem "manly" makes them feel small.

Their misguided belief system tells that all forms of worldly wealth, success, and status are "masculine traits," so they refuse to be with a woman whose very presence reminds them of their own lacking masculinity.

But worldly wealth, success, and status aren't manly, masculine traits, are they? At least they aren't in the religion of divine supremacy. They're simply divine favors of Allah.

They're Upset with Allah

The truth is, male supremacists are less angry with these highly accomplished women than they are angry with themselves and resentful toward Allah. Yes, you read that right. **This is really just thinly veiled *hasad* (spiritually destructive envy) dressed up as masculinity.**

How do we know the resentment is ultimately targeted at Allah? **Any worldly success that a human enjoys in this world, whether male or female, falls under the category of "favors of Allah."** This is something that Allah Himself tells us in the Qur'an.

Over and over, Allah reminds all human beings, male and female, of His divine prerogative: **He can bestow His favors on any of His servants that He chooses and to any extent that He chooses,** thereby allowing some people to excel others, whether in wealth, intelligence, status, skill, or anything else.

Allah also tells us that, when He does this, we should not covet a divine favor that He's given to someone else, no matter how much they exceed us in this world, most especially when that person being granted this divine favor is of the opposite gender. Incidentally, this very point is mentioned in a divine chapter translated as "The Women" in the Qur'an:

وَلَا تَتَمَنَّوْا مَا فَضَّلَ اللَّهُ بِهِ بَعْضَكُمْ عَلَىٰ بَعْضٍ لِّلرِّجَالِ نَصِيبٌ مِّمَّا اكْتَسَبُوا وَلِلنِّسَاءِ نَصِيبٌ مِّمَّا اكْتَسَبْنَ وَسْئَلُوا اللَّهَ مِن فَضْلِهِ إِنَّ اللَّهَ كَانَ بِكُلِّ شَيْءٍ عَلِيمًا ﴿٣٢﴾

"And do not covet (or wish for) that by which Allah has made some of you exceed others. For men is a share of what they have earned, and for women is a share of what they have earned. And ask Allah of His bounty. Indeed, Allah is ever, of all things, Knowing."
—*An-Nisaa* (4:32)

But male supremacist men feel like they're being wronged when Allah does exactly what He says going to do: whatever He wants. And this makes male supremacist men angry to the core.

Meanwhile, **all they had to do was follow Allah's instructions in the Qur'an: Ask Allah of His bounty.** Or, as the saying goes, ask and you shall receive.

But the problem is, male supremacists won't be content with only receiving divine favors for themselves. They want assurance that these same favors will be denied to women.

Twenty-three

Their Phobia of Feminism Leads to Sin

Here's something else you should know about male supremacists, especially the Muslims who identify with the male-centrism: **They fear feminism more than they fear Allah, and they hate feminism more than they love Islam.**

Naturally, this exists on a spectrum, so there are varying degrees of this hatred and fear. But here's how you can understand what's going on: A male supremacist's fear and hatred of feminism overtakes their commitment to Allah and Islam whenever they are faced with anything that resembles feminism in any way, even if that thing is from Islam itself.

Their hatred of feminism manifests as rejecting, denying, or minimizing any parts of Islam that overlap with feminism (e.g., women's rights in Islam, honoring women, protecting women from harm, showing compassion to women, allowing women freedom of choice in entering and leaving a marriage, supporting a woman's right to her own wealth, etc.). In this way, they hate feminism more than they love Islam, so much so that they are willing to leave off parts of their faith as a means to stay committed to hating feminism.

Their fear of feminism manifests as indulging in sin, evil, or dhulm (i.e., disobeying Islam) in an effort to fight against any evidence of feminism or anything that could even be *interpreted* as "feminist adjacent" (resembling feminism even if it isn't feminism in truth). One common example of this is harming, harassing, abusing, vilifying, or slandering any woman who shows signs of self-love that is divine-centered (vs. male-centered), being an "independent woman" (e.g., having a successful business), living life in a way that doesn't center a man, seeking a divorce, feeling content after divorce, supporting women heal from abuse, having standards for marriage that deny access to men she has no desire to marry, and the list goes on.

In this way, male supremacists are willing to rush headlong into sin with no fear of Allah whatsoever. This, so long as it allows them to engage in any act that can be thrown into the category of "fighting the evils of feminism." This is how they fear feminism more than they fear Allah.

Men of Taqwaa Love Islam and Fear Allah

Men (and women) who follow the Islamic model of religion (i.e., divine supremacy) place their love of Allah and Islam over everything and everyone, even their own nafs.

In those moments that they feel inclined toward sin or dhulm, as all children of Adam will from time to time, their fear of Allah intervenes on their behalf and returns them to the right path. They then immediately repent, self-correct, and remain committed to the health of their souls. This, even when this choice requires them to sit in the discomfort of hurt feelings, a wounded ego, swallowing their pride, or facing their inner darknesses and unhealed wounds (as we all have inner work to do until we die).

In the religion of divine supremacy, it is taqwaa and fear of Allah that guide the behavior of believers, even when facing public humiliation, heartbreak, or disrespect. In these moments, men of taqwaa in particular look to the example of the Prophet (peace be upon him).

Even when he was stressed out due to his wives' behavior, and even when he wasn't sure whether or not the rumors about his beloved wife Aisha (may Allah be pleased with her) were true, Prophet Muhammad ﷺ remained a kind, compassionate, safe person. In fact, in this latter moment of distress, despite his own hurt and uncertainty, he was deeply concerned with the health of Aisha's soul, hence his encouraging her to repent if the rumors were true.

Male Supremacists Prefer Misogyny Over the Sunnah

But male supremacist men do not look to the prophetic example to guide their ideas of manhood. They look to the Sunnah only when aspects of their *interpretation* of it align with their male-centric, anti-women '*aqeedah*.

This is where you'll find them quoting hadith about women prostrating to men, about men being superior to women, about women being deficient in their religion, and (one of their favorite) women's ingratitude to their husbands causing women to be the majority in the Hellfire.

In this, they ignore the rules of interpreting these texts, one of which would require them to recognize other, more established truths about the Hereafter. If they did this, they would realize that Muslim women couldn't possibly be the majority of Hellfire and that ingratitude to one's husband couldn't possibly be the worst sin.

This is because the Qur'an has made it undeniably clear that the majority of people in the Hellfire will be disbelievers, and that the most common sin resulting in this fate is *shirk* (worshipping other than Allah and assigning divine attributes to creation). In its major form, *shirk* is an unforgivable sin that results in a person entering Hellfire and never being granted access to Paradise. Yet this is the very sin male supremacists love and are eagerly calling to when they oppose divine supremacy in favor of male supremacy.

Here is relevant to mention something I mentioned in an earlier chapter regarding how their pathway to major *shirk* manifests:

In the Qur'an, Allah says:

$$\text{ٱتَّخَذُوٓا۟ أَحْبَارَهُمْ وَرُهْبَٰنَهُمْ أَرْبَابًا مِّن دُونِ ٱللَّهِ}$$

"They have taken their scholars [or rabbis and priests] and monks as lords besides Allah..."
—*At-Tawbah* (9:31)

It is narrated in a famous hadith that when 'Adee ibn Haatim, a prophetic Companion who had converted to Islam from Christianity, heard this *ayah* being recited, he said to the Prophet (peace be upon him): "We didn't worship them." The Prophet ﷺ responded, "Did they not make *haraam* (forbidden) what Allah had made *halaal* (permissible) and you made it *haraam* [too]? And did they not make *halaal* what Allah had made *haraam*, and you made it *halaal* [too]?" 'Adee replied, "Certainly." The Prophet ﷺ said, "That was how you worshipped them" (Al-Tirmidhi).

Therefore, when a woman is told she must abandon what she believes is *haraam* to follow what her husband believes is *halaal* or that she must abandon what she believes is *halaal* to follow what her husband believes in *haraam*, then according to the religion of Islam—which is based on divine supremacy, not male supremacy—she is being asked to worship her husband and take him as a god besides Allah, literally. This is the worst type of *shirk*, and it takes a person outside the fold of Islam.

Twenty-four

They Love Podcast-Branded Masculinity

One of the most popular manifestations of the deviant ideology of male supremacy today is the Red Pill cult. This cult ideology is the "sunnah of manhood" that male supremacists seek to emulate, and they often uphold it with more fervor than they do the Sunnah of the Prophet (peace be upon him).

The Red Pill cult is a fast-spreading male supremacist extremist cult that attracts unhealed, insecure men desperate to *feel like* men. Here, I emphasize the words "feel like" because **these men are less interested in *being* men than they are in *feeling like* men.** As such, they are unwilling and sometimes unable (due to their current unhealed states) to show up as real men of taqwaa in their own lives. So, they rely on an externalized form of masculinity that obligates women to act as conduits of masculinity on their behalf.

They Prefer Podcast Mics Over Inner Work

As alluded to earlier, the foundational *'aqeedah* of the Red Pill cult is *soo'u dhann* (applying the worst possible assumption or interpretation) of all things female. This is why they continuously choose podcast-branded masculinity (and social-media-branded femininity) over taqwaa-centered manhood (and womanhood), which is taught in the Qur'an and prophetic Sunnah.

Male supremacist men are scared to do the inner work that is required to show up as real men of taqwaa in this world. So, they take a shortcut to self-importance by tearing down women with the spiritual strength, personal success, and self-respect that they could only dream of in their unhealed states.

As aforementioned, they rush to call these self-respecting women "feminists." Or they resort to tearing down women whom they feel too insecure or worthless to stand next to as romantic partners. They call *these* women "low value."

What "Feminist" and "Low Value" Really Mean

As I touched on earlier, this is all projection, especially for men addicted to Red Pill ideology more than self-honesty. Now, keeping in mind *their* negative definition of feminism, which I discussed in an earlier chapter, and how it almost always equals something disconnected from Islam, know this:

"Feminist" is a projection of their own disconnect from Islam, which they project onto self-respecting, believing women who know their worth and their Islamic rights.

"Low value" is a projection of their own inner feelings of worthlessness, which they fear would surface if they chose a woman with enough self-awareness and life experience to challenge them to actually show up as real men of taqwaa in a relationship.

In other words, they are telling on themselves with what they call out in women. It's the classic psychology of tearing down something you don't feel worthy of having, or that you know will force you to level up in a way you're not ready or willing to.

This is also why **they rush to podcast mics faster than they run to therapy,** or even faster than they run to the prayer mat or open the Qur'an.

Twenty-five

Women Can Be Male Supremacists

B ut let's be honest. It's not just men who are male supremacists. Women are too. It's actually the go-to category for both men *and* women who are living with unhealed wounds. These are people who are seeking to hide their insecurities and refusals to improve themselves behind claims of being "masculine" or "feminine."

Sometimes they cloak their male supremacy behind claims of being "traditional," a term which (not surprisingly) doesn't fit easily or clearly into an Islamic context. Why? Because it doesn't really mean anything specific—except, of course, what male supremacist men and women arbitrarily *claim* it means.

Remember how I discussed male supremacists' random, knee-jerk use of the word feminist? And how they almost always attach to a negative connotation? Well, it's the same thing here with the word "traditional," but with the opposite intention: Male supremacists almost always apply to the word "traditional" a positive connotation, even when it's being used to block, shame, or guilt a woman away from an Islamic right, mercy, or halaal option that Allah has made available to her—and even when it's being used to praise a woman doing something contrary to Islamic guidance (e.g.,

"I never go to Islamic classes and learn my faith for myself. I follow my husband in everything, even if something doesn't make sense to me.")

If you remember how they hate feminism more than they love Islam, this use of the word "traditional" is a good example of that. Calling certain women "traditional" who prioritize blindly following their husbands in everything, even in matters of faith that all Muslims (male and female) are *obligated* to study and understand for themselves, allows male supremacist men and women to reject certain parts of Islam, namely those parts that require women to show up like full human beings responsible for their own souls in front of Allah.

But by calling this type of spiritual self-erasure in women "traditional," male supremacists are able to praise what goes against Islam and vilify what upholds Islam (e.g., a woman studying Islam for herself and taking full responsibility for her own soul).

But Can't Islam Be Called Traditional?

Islam deals mostly in *halaal* and *haraam* based on the Qur'an and the Prophetic Sunnah. As such, these divine texts naturally respect and honor personal choice so long as this personal choice does not contradict the texts.

Therefore, if someone (man or woman) wants to use the word "traditional" to describe certain parts of Islam, they are free to do so. Similarly, if someone (man or woman) wants to use the word "feminist" to describe certain parts of Islam, they too are free to do so. In both cases, the requirement for using either worldly term would be that *your* definition does not contradict Islamic principles.

After you've established and clarified what you mean by the term, there's nothing wrong with using either term in the way you prefer, even if someone else is using that exact term in a way that contradicts Islam.

Unfortunately, however, **so much that is labeled "traditional Islam" is really just Islamicized male supremacist ideology,** especially as it relates to discussions on a woman's role in marriage.

Male Supremacist Women Fear Self-Love

Just like male supremacist men fear female self-love, so do male supremacist women. But this fear is often carefully hidden behind the claim of being a "traditional woman." Naturally, there's nothing wrong with getting married and then sacrificing certain hobbies and life goals you once had before marriage, but there *is* something wrong with claiming that all women have to.

Male supremacists want us to believe that we're being "good Muslim women" when we give up our talents, hide our intelligence, and run away from worldly success. However, when we believe the lie that they tell us about none of these things mattering to them in a wife, here's what's really happening: We've just accepted an invitation to fulfill the impossible task of protecting the fragile ego of an unhealed, insecure man who externalizes his masculinity.

But a male supremacist man will never feel like a man until he decides to actually be one. And this requires him taking it upon himself to look within his own nafs (inner self) and choose manhood. Then he must learn what manhood actually means in Islam.

In Islam (i.e. divine supremacy), manhood is soul-centered and is rooted in taqwaa (God-consciousness, self-discipline, and secure masculinity). It has absolutely nothing to do with making sure your wife stays small so you feel big, and it has absolutely nothing to do with feeling superior to women in *everything* of this world.

Choosing Podcast-Branded Femininity

Like male supremacist men addicted to podcast-branded masculinity, many male supremacist women choose love and belonging on podcast mics, too—or through social-media branded femininity. This, instead of seeking healing and self-betterment through therapy, spiritual autonomy, and soul-nourishing self-love.

The Red Pill podcast culture is a mental space that allows self-proclaimed "traditional women" to feel superior to women that male supremacist men tear down in their podcasts. It's also where some Red Pill women feel free to tear down self-loving, believing women who have more courage and self-respect than they do.

Meanwhile, as they slander Allah's female servants due to their own feelings of female worthlessness, they feel like good, pious Muslim women. Why? Because they genuinely think that **if men are pleased with their words, then Allah is pleased with their words.**

This is how male supremacy works in the minds of those committed to it.

I Had to Heal, Too

If I'm being honest, in many ways, before I made the conscious choice to heal, I myself was influenced by fear of self-love and admiration of performative womanhood.

And, truth be told, letting go of this fake femininity under the guise of being a "traditional woman" wasn't easy. And though I hate to admit it, some parts of this journey of detoxing from male supremacy and embracing taqwaa-centered femininity and self-love remain difficult to let go of till today.

Why? Because if there's one thing that performative womanhood offers you, it's the decreased likelihood of being on the receiving end of slander and personal attacks by your brothers (and sisters) in faith, many of whom live under the Western model of religion (male supremacy) instead of the Islamic model of religion (divine supremacy).

Twenty-six

Women Aren't Innocent! They Say

One of the reactions I typically get when I'm discussing what Muslim women have suffered under Islamicized male supremacy is something like: "You're acting like women are these perfect, sinless creatures and ideal wives, but they aren't innocent!"

And my response to that is this: Obviously.

That's precisely the point.

They're human—just like men.

Men aren't god-like "kings," and women aren't robot-like "servants." *SubhaanAllah*.

What part of this don't we understand?

Women Need Room to Be Fully Human

Anas ibn Malik (may Allah be pleased with him) reported that the Prophet (peace and blessings be upon him) said, "All of the children of Adam sin, and the best of those who sin are those who constantly repent" (Sunan al-Tirmidhī 2499, *Sahih* by Al-Suyuti).

One of the many problems with male supremacy is that it doesn't allow women the room to be full, flawed human beings with complex lives and struggles, just like the sons of Adam. They teach us that the daughters of Adam can't be

136

trusted with life's challenges like other adults, so they should be kept locked up in their homes and treated like a robotic house appliance, with a wife-mother programming feature preset to "servant mode" 24-7.

It simply doesn't make any sense, especially considering that this human-robot "house appliance" is expected to be a source of constant emotional support, compassion, and forgiveness to everyone but herself. Moreover, in her robot mode, she's expected to see everyone, most especially her husband and other men in the world, as fully worthy of compassion, forgiveness, and the overlooking of faults. That is, everyone in the world is worthy of this except herself and other women.

Here is where male supremacists borrow from the doctrine of divine supremacy when it means letting men off the hook for being flawed and sinful (or even downright abusive), then they rush back to the doctrine of male supremacy the moment that they are tasked with extending women the same courtesy.

So, no, this most certainly isn't about fighting for women to be viewed as innocent and sinless. That would be signing up for just another version of the *same* problem we're facing with male supremacy. **This is about fighting for women to be viewed (and treated) as full human beings.** But it shouldn't even be a fight at all.

In the end, this is about re-embracing the Qur'anic and Sunnah view of humanity that we learn in divine supremacy, where all children of Adam (male and female) sin and fall short, where all children of Adam have access to the divine gift of Allah's mercy and forgiveness, and where all children of Adam have a direct, one-on-one relationship with their Creator with no intermediaries between them and Allah.

But male supremacy teaches us that this one-on-one, direct relationship between Allah and His servants is a mercy offered only to men. Women, especially in the context of fulfilling the role of wife in marriage, are blocked from it unless a man gives her permission or says he's pleased with her.

In other words, male supremacy teaches us that Tawheed (worshipping Allah alone and having a personal relationship with Him) is the spiritual path for men in this world, while *shirk* (worshipping their husbands as the foundational means of accessing Allah) is the spiritual path for women in this world.

But ultimately, both of these paths end up in *shirk*, because asking someone to worship you while you worship Allah contradicts Tawheed just as certainly as bowing to a physical idol does.

Of course, as aforementioned, all of this exists on a spectrum, and not all levels of male supremacy land us in major *shirk*. But even on its most "innocent" level, it teaches women to engage in the sin of minor *shirk*. This happens through requiring a woman to filter all her choices through whether or not a man will be pleased with her before she even considers whether Allah will be pleased with her. And this indoctrination into *riyaa'* begins before a woman is even married.

"Traditional Women" Need to Be Careful

For women who consider themselves "traditional women" but have been indoctrinated into male supremacist ideology over the Sunnah of divine supremacy, there is a hefty cost to pay. And that is a nafs living in constant victim mode.

Victim mode allows a woman to never take full accountability for the state of her own life or soul. It also allows her to justify all her actions (or inactions) as a female servant of Allah, so long as she can claim that whatever she was doing was in the service of pleasing her husband or performing for the male gaze.

Becoming aware of when you're falling into the sin of *riyaa'* itself requires deep introspection and consistent inner work. This is because recognizing when you are either doing something for other than the pleasure of Allah or when you are withholding yourself from doing something that would please Allah isn't easy. Both of these blind spots fall under the category of *riyaa'*, which is a type of minor *shirk*, and here, it's important to understand that "minor" only means that it doesn't take you outside the fold of Islam. It doesn't mean that this type of *shirk* is trivial to Allah.

Ma'qil ibn Yasar (may Allah be pleased with him) said:

"I departed with Abu Bakr to meet the Prophet, peace and blessings be upon him, and the Prophet said, "**O Abu Bakr, there is idolatry (*shirk*) among you more hidden than the crawling of an ant.**" Abu Bakr said, "Is there idolatry other than to make a god alongside Allah?" The Prophet said, "**By the One in whose hand is my soul, there is idolatry more hidden than the crawling of an ant. Shall I not tell you something to say to rid you of it, both minor and major? Say: O Allah, I seek refuge in You that I associate partners with You while I know, and I seek Your forgiveness for what I do not know**" (*Al-Adab al-Mufrad lil-Bukhāri* 715, *Sahih* by Al-Albaani).

For women, this sin becomes all the more challenging to recognize because, as a general rule, pleasing and serving our husbands *is* pleasing to Allah. However, there are limits, and the most obvious limit is that you cannot disobey Allah or harm your own soul in the process.

But how can you know what's harming you if you're disconnected from yourself and your most intimate personal and spiritual needs on the altar of being a "traditional woman"?

Victimhood Is a Path to Hellfire

Here, as women, we need to understand that deconstructing male supremacy and detoxing all traces of it from our *nafs* isn't just a preferable option. It's an obligation. And if we don't do this, then we are risking having no excuse in front of Allah on the Day of Judgment when we fall into *shirk*.

This is especially the case if we've taken our husbands (and other men) as gods besides Allah through allowing them to dictate *halaal* and *haraam* to us, either while we know the truth is different in front of Allah or while we make no effort to learn our *deen* (spiritual way of life) for ourselves, and then using as an excuse that we're blindly following our husbands or other men in our life.

No, there's nothing wrong with trusting someone who has more knowledge than you in certain matters. But there is something very wrong with *intentionally* remaining ignorant of your *deen* and then dying while having had no knowledge of parts of your faith that Allah had made accessible to you, even as a non-scholar.

One thing I remind the sisters in Feminine Soul Reset is this: **Both entitlement *and* victimhood are paths to the Hellfire.** Moreover, ultimately, these are just two sides of the same coin, as both are about running from accountability in life. This is because in both cases, you are placing on the shoulders of someone else what you should be doing for your own life and soul. For men, this manifests as using women as conduits of their masculinity, and for women, this manifests as fully accepting this passive, self-erasing role in life and faith.

To understand just how deep this is, we can look at the Qur'an, where we learn about different types and levels of *dhulm* (wrongdoing), all of which can land a person in the Hellfire. This is because it's not only obvious dhulm (oppression, abuse, and feeling entitled to harm others) that can subject us to punishment in the Hereafter. Toxic victimhood can too.

In fact, toxic victimhood in itself is a type of *dhulm*, as it equates to wronging your own soul. And when we do this, especially after having been called away from this spiritually destructive path, our punishment in the Hereafter (may Allah protect us) is little different from the ones who shamed and guilted us into doing it, especially if our passivity has reached the level of major *shirk* (e.g., following our husband when he says something is *halaal* that we know is *haraam* or vice versa).

In the Qur'an, Allah says:

كُلَّمَا دَخَلَتْ أُمَّةٌ لَّعَنَتْ أُخْتَهَا حَتَّى إِذَا ادَّارَكُوا فِيهَا جَمِيعًا قَالَتْ أُخْرَاهُمْ لِأُولَاهُمْ رَبَّنَا هَـٰؤُلَاءِ أَضَلُّونَا فَآتِهِمْ عَذَابًا ضِعْفًا مِّنَ النَّارِ قَالَ لِكُلٍّ ضِعْفٌ وَلَـٰكِن لَّا تَعْلَمُونَ ﴿٣٨﴾

"...Every time a nation enters [the Fire], it will curse its sister-people [who went before] until, when they have all overtaken one another therein, the last of them will say about the first of them, 'Our Lord, these had misled us, so give them a double punishment of the Fire.' He will say, 'Double for all.' But this you do not understand."
—Al-Aa'raaf (7:38)

Twenty-seven
Women in Divine Supremacy vs. Male Supremacy

So we can think of male supremacist men's oppression, entitlement, and abuse of women as *dhulm* in the masculine, and we can think of male supremacist women's toxic victimhood, passive helplessness, and self-erasure as *dhulm* in the feminine.

In front of Allah, as it relates to any human soul (male or female), knowingly neglecting the spiritual health of your soul is a path to Hellfire. It doesn't matter whether our spiritual self-neglect manifested as *dhulm* in the masculine in this world or whether it manifested as *dhulm* in the feminine. It's intentional spiritual self-neglect all the same. In this way, they are effectively one and the same.

This is why having a healthy relationship with yourself and your Creator is essential in this world, especially for women. I say "especially for women" because we are the one gender that is fought from all sides, even from within our own homes.

This is because, in male supremacy, it is both self-serving and ego-boosting for the men in charge of our protection to make us believe that neglecting ourselves and ignoring the deepest needs of our souls is equal to piety or praiseworthy sacrifice "for the sake of Allah." And unfortunately, even men who identify most with divine supremacy in almost every area of their lives will suddenly prefer male supremacy when it comes to how they lead their households and treat their wives and children. So, even otherwise "good men" find it difficult to resist the addictive "power rush" of having their wife submit to them in *everything*, even when she's quite obviously suffering as a result and even in matters that should be between her and Allah.

For this reason, it is all the more pertinent for us as women to ensure that our relationship with our soul and Allah takes priority over all other relationships, most especially the one we have with our husbands. For it is in this intimate, soul companionship of marriage that so many of us lose our way—and ourselves.

We're Spiritually Equal to Men

As alluded to in the previous chapter, both men and women are complex, imperfect human beings. As such, just like men, women are full of flaws and imperfections, and they struggle with sin and dhulm (wronging their souls) just like the male children of Adam.

As women, we are not different creatures from men. We are the same creation. In fact, we are literally *of* each other. Our Mother Aisha (may Allah be pleased with her) reported that **the Messenger of Allah ﷺ said, "Verily, women are the counterparts of men"** (*Sunan al-Tirmidhī* 113, Sahih by Al-Albaani). Regarding this prophetic hadith, the Imam al-Khattabi commented:

> **"His saying that 'women are counterparts of men' means their equals and their likeness in creation and nature, as if they split off from men.** In jurisprudence, it is an affirmation of the principle of analogy and

equivalence in rulings, same by same, such that if the address is conveyed in the male grammatical form, it is also addressed to women, except for special topics whose specification is established by evidence" (Ma'ālim al-Sunan 1/79).

It is male supremacy that seeks to strip women of their humanity, which is the natural humanness that is decreed by Allah and taught by His Messenger ﷺ regarding all human souls (male and female).

Male supremacists achieve this by fixating on the different roles and degrees of responsibilities between men and women and then concluding that these differences, especially that of men's assignment of *qawwaamah* and the fact that "only four women" reached perfection, are indicative of a fundamental inequality between men and women. They claim that this inequality means that women inherently "inferior" and men inherently "superior."

Among other things, they also do this by viewing the "superior" spiritual perfection of prophets (who were men) through the lens of gender vs. through the lens of taqwaa. As such, in male supremacy, prophetic superiority is less about these men fulfilling a superior divine assignment from Allah than about them being men. Then male supremacists conclude that all men have a similar element of "inherent superiority" inside them by birthright.

Even if we prefer to use the English term "superior" to describe men's divine assignment of leadership on earth, as well as their degree of responsibility over women, our test in front of Allah is simply this: What does this mean in practical reality? What does this mean in spiritual reality? And most significantly, **what does this belief in "superior men" do to our souls?**

For men, if you find that this understanding of your faith and of your unique divine assignment inspires in you taqwaa,

144

humility, and heart-trembling fear of Allah, as well as a heart free from *kibr* (pride)—especially in how you show up in fulfilling your obligations toward women—then by all means, think of yourself as superior. As with all English words that are not perfect translations of meaning from the Qur'anic Arabic or prophetic narrations, so long as this word conveys to your heart what Allah intended to convey to your heart when He revealed it, then it's no problem at all what term you prefer.

But I suspect that for most men, humility and taqwaa, as well as deep fear of Allah in their treatment of women, are not the effects that this word "superior" has on their minds and hearts. And Allah knows us better than we know our own selves. So, be careful when you claim that it is Allah who wants you to call yourself "superior," especially when this term incites boasting superiority in front of women while abandoning doing good, acting right, and fostering peace between men and women.

In the Qur'an, Allah says:

وَلَا تَجْعَلُواْ ٱللَّهَ عُرْضَةً لِّأَيْمَٰنِكُمْ أَن تَبَرُّواْ وَتَتَّقُواْ
وَتُصْلِحُواْ بَيْنَ ٱلنَّاسِ وَٱللَّهُ سَمِيعٌ عَلِيمٌ ﴿٢٢٤﴾

"And make not Allah's [name] an excuse in your oaths against doing good, or acting rightly, or making peace between people; and Allah is Hearing and Knowing."
—*Al-Baqarah* (2:224)

Furthermore, when it comes to using the word "superior" to describe who men are in front of Allah, it's also helpful to go back to the first two questions I asked in relation to why it's so often preferred to describe men in comparison to women: What does this mean in practical reality? What does this mean in spiritual reality?

Are we saying that in practical, spiritual reality, if a man does a good deed, then the reward that is written in his Book of Deeds is multiplied to such an extent that is denied to a woman doing that same good deed? Are we saying that when a man commits a sin that Allah is more accepting of his evil and disobedience in comparison to a woman doing the same sin? Are we saying that when Allah loves any of His servants (male or female), then some of that love is automatically withheld before He bestows it on a woman?

If so, what is our proof? If not, what is your point?

Twenty-eight

Dark Truths About Male Supremacy

O ne of the dark sides of male supremacy is that it almost always leads to the sin of misogyny, a serious *dhulm* that is warned against in both the Qur'an and prophetic Sunnah (e.g., **"A believing man should not hate a believing woman..."** [Sahih Muslim]).

In the Qur'an, Allah says:

$$\text{وَإِذَا ٱلۡمَوۡءُۥدَةُ سُئِلَتۡ ۝ بِأَىِّ ذَنۢبٍ قُتِلَتۡ ۝}$$

"And when the female [who was] buried alive is asked, For what crime she was killed?"
—*At-Takweer* (81:8-9)

The clear implication here is: Are we claiming that by the mere fact that someone is born female, that she is deserving of all sorts of harm and abuse? This is no small matter to Allah. Why? Because Allah hates all dhulm (wrongdoing and oppression), no matter the gender of the target.

As such, none of Allah's servants should be subjected to unnecessary harm, annoyance, or irritation (as so many women are subjected to in these Last Days), especially when they've done nothing to deserve this. It's not only men who deserve to live their lives in peace.

In the Qur'an, Allah says:

وَٱلَّذِينَ يُؤْذُونَ ٱلْمُؤْمِنِينَ وَٱلْمُؤْمِنَٰتِ بِغَيْرِ مَا ٱكْتَسَبُواْ فَقَدِ ٱحْتَمَلُواْ بُهْتَٰنًا وَإِثْمًا مُّبِينًا ۝

"And those who cause harm (or annoyance or irritation) to believing men and believing women for [anything] other than what they have earned (i.e., while they've done nothing to deserve this) have certainly born upon themselves a slander and manifest sin."
—*Al-Ahzaab* (33:58)

As for all the harassment, abuse, and social lynching that many believing women endure from male supremacist men (e.g., slandering divorced women, attacking women for speaking out against narcissistic abuse, accusing women of being misandrists if they caution against male-worship, etc.), **what exactly did these female servants of Allah do to deserve all of this?**

This is something that male supremacists should sit with, especially as every breath they take is a countdown to when their souls will be extracted and their bodies will be lowered beneath the ground. At that moment, there will be no time for repentance, and you're left with only the good and bad you brought upon yourself in this world.

Truly "Superior Men" Don't Need to Boast

Unfortunately, so much misogyny is defended by pointing to religious "evidence" that says men are superior.

As discussed in the previous chapter, it's no problem if we genuinely believe that the English word "superior" (with all its connotations) is the best translation of what Allah intends to convey in the Arabic. However, when we find men going to great lengths to boast about their "superiority" —and to the very people who should be experiencing their "superior" protection, compassion, and good treatment (if the men themselves believe this superiority to be true)—this is indicative of men living contrary to taqwaa and true faith, not to mention an obviously "inferior" spiritual mindset.

Even when there is no doubt about the superiority of someone in comparison to others, like Prophet Muhammad ﷺ in comparison to all other men, including other prophets, we're not even allowed to go around boasting about this to others, especially when our intention is only to convey, "We're better than you!"

For example, when a Muslim argued with a Jew and claimed the Prophet Muhammad was better than Prophet Moses (peace be upon them), the Prophet is described as becoming so angry that anger was apparent on his face. He then said, **"Do not give superiority to any prophet [over another] amongst God's prophets..."** (Bukhari).

This, even when we know for a fact, as mentioned in the Qur'an, that Allah has indeed given certain prophets a status above others. **How much more so when *non-prophets* are bragging about their (alleged) superiority over other servants of Allah?** Especially when these very servants do not even know if they will die with emaan in their hearts, let alone if they'll be granted a higher station in Paradise than they imagine they're superior to.

The Lizard's Hole of Misogyny

Undoubtedly, the Western model of religion in nearly all its forms, including white supremacy and male supremacy, afflicts its people with a superiority complex.

As a result, Muslim lands and other areas of the world populated by people the West deems inferior, whether due to their "inferior" race or creed, are ravaged by destruction, persecution, and oppression. It is only the people who give up their own sense of identity and follow the West, and thus proclaim its superiority, that are protected from the worst levels of targeted harm.

In the context of marriage, male supremacy, though on a much smaller scale, operates similarly, as it will naturally remain committed to the religious model from which it was born. In this male-centric religious model, **women are placed in one of two categories:**

1) righteous and pure
2) corrupt and evil.

However, **women's righteousness and evil are not based on their relationship with Allah, but on their relationship with a man.**

When Muslims (men and women) embrace this male supremacist Western model of religion, they are simply choosing the infamous "lizard's hole" as prophesied in this famous hadith:

"Verily, you will follow the path of those before you, step by step and inch by inch; [such that] if they entered the hole of a lizard, you would follow." We (the Companions) said, "O Messenger of Allah, do you mean the Jews and Christians?" The Prophet ﷺ said, "Who else?" (Ṣaḥīḥ al-Bukhārī 3269, Ṣaḥīḥ Muslim 2669).

Women in Divine Supremacy vs. Male Supremacy

In divine supremacy, which is the Islamic model of religion, a woman is simply a human being who is a female child of Adam. Therefore, she shows up in the world similar to a male child of Adam.

As a result, as mentioned in an earlier chapter, she has moral struggles and human imperfections just like a man does, hence the famous prophetic hadith telling us that *all* children of Adam (male and female) fall into sin.

However, **in male supremacist ideology, a woman is tasked with showing up in a way that is equivalent to a flawless "angel," or she is cast into the category of a corrupt "devil."** Muslim male supremacists might not use this exact terminology, but they uphold its unreasonable meaning, nonetheless.

Consequently, for the woman being judged by the angel-devil standards, there is very little (if any) nuance in between. Moreover, **her flawlessness or corruption is viewed entirely through one lens: her desirability or usefulness to a man.** This is because, in male supremacy, servicing and pleasing a man is viewed as a woman's purpose in life.

In divine supremacy, on the other hand, a woman's purpose in life is to serve and worship Allah alone. If in her servitude to Allah, she chooses to get married and earn extra blessings as a wife, this is a personal choice that aligns with her higher purpose. It is not her higher purpose in itself.

In male supremacy, the "angelic" women are not the women who dedicate their lives to serving Allah. These are women who eagerly serve the needs and desires of men, and without complaint. Most preferably, the angelic woman serves a man while displaying no needs or desires of her own.

In contrast, in male supremacy, "devilish" women are those who show up with human flaws, a sinful past (or present), or a desire for any life path outside servitude to a man. This is why male supremacist cults like Red Pill often refer to women as "low value" or "damaged goods." They view every woman as property of a man, and they assess her as such, even when the woman is unmarried or not even seeking a relationship with a man.

In divine supremacy, every woman (like every man) is the "property" of Allah alone. Additionally, divine supremacy is rooted in *husnu dhann* (applying the best possible assumption or interpretation) to the choices and life paths of all Allah's servants, male and female.

In contrast, as previously mentioned, male supremacy is rooted in *soo'u dhann* (applying the worst possible assumption or interpretation) to women's lives, especially those women who are not obviously centering and serving men.

Twenty-nine

Misogyny Isn't What You Think

M ale supremacy's view of women is the very essence of misogyny. However, this is a concept most of us have misunderstood. This is because we likely think that misogyny simply means a *feeling* of hatred toward women. But it's so much deeper and more complex than that.

We're Seriously Misunderstanding Misogyny

Misogyny isn't just "hating women." **Misogyny is the view that women are superhuman and subhuman at once.**

To understand what this looks like in practical reality, we can go back to our discussion on how male supremacists see women, in essence, as either "angels" or "devils." These labels imply the "performance review" criteria based on the male gaze. In this way, **women are robbed of their right to a complex human experience.**

Let's look at an example. What happens when women sin and do bad things, especially while fulfilling their role as wives to their husbands (as they most certainly will because they're children of Adam)? In male supremacy, men don't automatically think women are simply struggling, imperfect human beings, just like they are, and thus need compassion, understanding, and forgiveness. Rather, they conclude that she is a corrupt, disobedient wife; that she is acting on some inherent evil or female deficiency inside her; or that she is merely an ungrateful, "unrighteous woman."

In this mental space, it's hard to imagine that these men, even during their private, heartfelt supplications to Allah, take time to sincerely mention their wives, beseeching Allah for her forgiveness and self-betterment—or for their own softness of heart toward her.

On the other hand, when a man sins and does bad things, even in his role as a husband to his wife, male supremacists view this a just a natural, inevitable part of life. They see their mistakes and even obvious wrongdoings as things that all men do or struggle with. Consequently, they tell themselves that these are things that any "good woman" would accept (or at least be patient with), forgive, and overlook—no matter how egregious *their* crime.

Thus, this is the unwritten (and widely accepted) rule in male supremacy: **Only men are entitled to a loving, supportive, unwavering, dedicated romantic partner at all times**. This, even when these men are drowning in obvious sin, or delving into it unapologetically.

For a woman, it's the exact opposite. In male supremacy, if a woman shows evidence of drowning in obvious sin, let alone delving into it unapologetically, she is cast off as some horrible, evil creature. And nearly every man (and woman) around him would agree with him.

However, even for the woman who shows no signs of sin, she is still robbed of her humanity in her role as a wife. Why? Because she is tasked with being superhuman. This superhuman role requires her to not only never fall into obvious sin, but also to display superhuman mental strength.

In this "superwoman" space, this "good woman" is a constant support system to her husband. She rushes to forgive and pardon her husband's *every* wrong, even his most reprehensible actions (private and public). She serves her husband morning and night while never tiring of pleasing and serving him. And she does all this without showing (or even *feeling*) the slightest frustration.

This "good woman" also must have superhuman emotional strength, as well as superhuman faith. This woman is fully accepting of *any* choice her husband makes, as he is the leader. She submits to whatever he chooses, and she does it with a smile, even when he chooses something as deeply hurtful as marrying another wife. Here, she isn't permitted to show or express the slightest anguish, lest she lose her "good woman" status.

Obviously, this type of "superhuman mode" in a relationship is both preposterous and unsustainable for *any* child of Adam. Even the self-proclaimed strong, superior men of male supremacy, who boast about not carrying the same emotional and religious "deficiencies" as women, wouldn't even *attempt* this level of perfect-husband mode. They know it's not even humanly possible or sensible.

Yet, oddly, that doesn't stop them from demanding it of women. Moreover, any woman unable (or unwilling) to show up as a man's dedicated "angel" and Marvel-like superhero support system is swiftly cast into the category of "low value" or "unrighteous wife." Or she's described as "not a real woman."

Worse still, the ridiculously impossible nature of the task doesn't stop women from naively believing they can be this superwoman.

If I'm being honest, I myself, in my youth, like so many other gullible young women before me, imagined I could "do it all." Thus, I tried to be "superwoman" to my husband for years.

And I paid mightily for it.

I nearly lost my life and my faith on that altar. Today, by the mercy of Allah, I'm reclaiming my life, health, and joy, as I detox from male supremacy and reintroduce the Islamic model of religion into my life.

Thirty

Choosing Marriage or Faith

I *didn't know another way of living existed,* I wrote in my journal some time ago, *at least not one that wouldn't cast me as guilty of selfishness, sin, and disregard for the rights others had over me. It took nearly losing my life and faith—along with a compassionate but firm warning from my doctor—before I took an honest look at the choices I had been repeatedly making in the name of faith, family, and love.*

Given how widespread and pervasive male supremacy is in these Last Days, even amongst some of our most celebrated and trusted imams, scholars, and community leaders, it's no surprise that more and more women feel compelled to choose between the soul companionship of marriage and the spiritual health of their souls.

And this is no small decision.

Many women who try to choose both find that they must compromise their relationship with Allah and their souls to maintain even the *semblance* of a healthy, long-lasting relationship with a man.

Other women try hard to commit themselves to the darkness of male supremacy, even the part that requires them to hate women. But they tell themselves that this male-centric, anti-women religious practice is "traditional Islam" or proof they're following the way of our pious predecessors. These women often repeat what male supremacist men say about "non-traditional" women, often calling them bitter, especially if they are divorced and content.

Tragically, however, this is all projection, as no real happiness can be found in a relationship built on male supremacy and female self-erasure. Reflecting on this sad reality, I'm reminded of something I wrote in my journal some time ago: *You'll notice that the most unhappy, bitter women are male supremacist women stuck in marriages with male supremacist men while telling themselves that it's love and they're righteous wives. But they call YOU bitter and toxic in order to convince themselves they made the right choice in giving up nearly everything that mattered to them, including themselves.*

Then there are those women at the beginning of their paths of love and faith. These are often women who unknowingly married into male supremacy, having been chosen due to their naivety, lacking self-love, or fresh trauma wounds; yet they thought they signed up for lasting love, emotional connection, and masculine protection. When they and their husbands first met, she genuinely thought she'd found her soul mate.

These are the women you meet years or even months after they got married (or became Muslim), and you can tell the zeal has left their hearts and that the light has dimmed in their eyes. And you can already see on their face the question that they themselves probably haven't even formed into words: *"Can I face another day?"*

It's one of the most heartbreaking things to witness.

Fortunately, by the mercy of Allah, there do exist those rare "Muslim love stories." This is where both the man and the woman love Allah and each other, where both the man and the woman are committed to the other's joy and self-betterment, and where both the man and the women each day invest in healthy self-love and in showing compassion to each other. All this they do while upholding the spiritual principles of divine supremacy.

While these stories of healthy, soul-nourishing love are few and far between, they are not unheard of. And here, I'm not talking about fairytale love. I'm talking about healthy, spiritually nourishing love. I'm talking about how all our "love stories" should look.

Not because I read too many romance novels or watched too many "happily ever after" movies. But because I often read and reflect on the Qur'an.

And I believe my Merciful Rabb, Al-Haqq, when He says:

$$\text{وَمِنْ ءَايَـٰتِهِۦٓ أَنْ خَلَقَ لَكُم مِّنْ أَنفُسِكُمْ أَزْوَٰجًا لِّتَسْكُنُوٓا۟ إِلَيْهَا}$$

$$\text{وَجَعَلَ بَيْنَكُم مَّوَدَّةً وَرَحْمَةً ۚ إِنَّ فِى ذَٰلِكَ لَءَايَـٰتٍ لِّقَوْمٍ}$$

$$\text{يَتَفَكَّرُونَ ﴿٢١﴾}$$

"And among His Signs is this, that He created for you mates from among yourselves, so that you may dwell in tranquility with them, and He has put affection [love] and mercy between your [hearts]. Verily, in that are Signs for those who reflect."
—*Ar-Room* (30:21)

This is how love in the soul companionship of marriage looks in divine supremacy.

May we all taste this part of the sweetness of emaan.

Epilogue

I Finally Learned Self-Love

I had to learn self-love, and it wasn't easy. I know now that part of the reason it was so hard for me to learn self-love was that it was constantly treated as something inappropriate or even sinful in Muslim circles, at least for the female soul. For some reason, so many Muslims had a phobia of self-love in women.

I was no different.

It was like, in order to be a good Muslim, especially a good Muslim *woman*, you had to go out of your way to prove that you *didn't* love yourself. You had to go out of your way to prove that you were willing to shrink and self-erase and sacrifice to the point of exhaustion so that men were happy and fulfilled, especially your husband.

As for myself, I took this to heart so much that I nearly lost myself in shrinking, self-erasing, and sacrificing. Only to find myself barely holding on to my faith and emotional wellness years later. But let me tell you what I eventually learned the hard way...

Self-Love Is a Superpower

Yes, you read that right.

I now see self-love as a superpower. Not like in the Marvel movies. But in the reality and possibilities for your own life.

When you have self-love, there's very little harm that others can bring you in this world—even if the harm stems from your own nafs (inner self).

Here's why: Self-love is more than loving and choosing yourself in romantic relationships. Self-love is loving and choosing your SOUL at all times.

This is why...

Reading the Qur'an each day is self-love.

Reading Surah Al-Kahf every Friday is self-love.

Praying every Salaah every day on time is self-love.

Spending a few more seconds in *sujood* is self-love.

Making du'aa for yourself and your sisters and brothers in faith is self-love.

Getting up for Qiyaam-ul-Layl (the Night Prayer) in the last third of the night is self-love.

And being compassionate with yourself—while gently and firmly holding yourself accountable—whenever you fall short in any of these is self-love.

This is how self-love is also part of emaan (sincere faith).

But the truth is, I learned all this after nearly losing my faith trying to please others at the expense of myself.

You know what changed everything, though? You know what made me finally choose myself? You know the one part of self-love that helped me heal from years of religious trauma and spiritual heartbreak?

Letting go of Islamicized male supremacy and then re-embracing true Islamic Tawheed (monotheism) into my life. This is a path rooted in divine supremacy, where Allah is the center of my life and heart, not restlessly seeking the pleasure of a man.

But Do You Feel Safe with Him?

10 REASONS

Why Performing Femininity Never Works *in* Love

Umm Zakiyyah

He Wanted a Feminine Wife and Daughters

"I just feel so blessed to be here," she said, averting her eyes nervously.

Quietly, we listened. We were a group of about twenty women, mostly non-Arab, and it was our first day at a small neighborhood Qur'an school in Riyadh, Saudi Arabia. At the time, I was living as an American expat there teaching English in the mornings and early afternoons and then studying Qur'an and Arabic in the late afternoons and evenings.

"I wasn't allowed to study Qur'an before I came here," she said, her voice shaking a bit. "None of us were."

"What do you mean?" we asked. "None of who?"

"The girls," she said. "The women," she added. "My father didn't allow it." She explained that along with herself, neither her mother nor any of her sisters or female relatives were allowed to read, study, or memorize the Qur'an.

The room grew silent momentarily.

"But why?" I asked, unable to contain myself.

"My father said girls don't need an education because they don't need it for marriage," she explained. "So, growing up, we were only allowed to learn things like cooking and cleaning, and we were forbidden to learn to read, or study books or anything like that."

"Not even the Qur'an?" I said, shocked.

She shook her head sadly. "No, but it's like that in our whole village. None of the girls are allowed."

Wow. I didn't even know what to say to that.

"But *alhamdulillaah*, my husband lets me study Qur'an."

The words "lets me" incited in me a complicated mixture of emotions that I wouldn't be able to name for many years, but at that moment, I stayed silent, listening intently and disturbed greatly.

"That's why I feel so blessed to be here," she continued. "I'm thankful to my husband for taking us out of our country and moving us here." Some of us asked what country she and her husband had moved from, and she said Afghanistan.

"But if your husband supports you, why did you have to leave your country to study Qur'an?" I asked.

"He could get into a lot of trouble with my father and the other men there," she explained. "So, we decided it's best for him to just pretend like he agrees with them until we could leave and come here." A hint of a smile formed on her face. "And now, I can finally learn to read," she said, joyful gratitude in those words.

The bittersweet sadness that settled over the room that day—and in my heart—is something I don't think I'll ever forget.

Not Exactly a Rare Exception

At the time that I'm writing this, it has been over fifteen years since I sat in that circle of women in Riyadh, Saudi Arabia. Yet it wasn't until one early morning about five years ago after I had long since returned home to the United States of America that I actually cried about it for the first time.

I was sitting in the prayer room of my Maryland townhome that day and reciting aloud from the very *mus'haf* (all-Arabic Qur'an) that I'd held in my hands the day that I listened to the Afghani woman share her story. It was then that it all came back to me suddenly.

The tears flowed from a deep place inside me. It was a carefully hidden place in my *nafs* that had sheltered my own spiritual heartbreak and emotional wounding for years. And it was only in that moment that I could cry because before then, I wasn't broken or brave enough to even acknowledge that it was there.

I cried because I felt in that moment the heavy grief I had been carrying, which was a weighty mixture of my own grief and the Afghani woman's, as well as the grief of so many Muslim girls and women who didn't even know they had lost something worth grieving—or that they needed someone to cry for them.

I cried, too, because not enough girls or women understood until it was too late that the story of the Afghani woman (and of her husband who'd be severely punished and socially ostracized for supporting her) is not a rare exception, though we'd like so very much for it to be. No, *we* likely will never be forbidden from learning to read or write or to memorize the Qur'an. Nevertheless, every day we internalize harmful messages about ourselves and what it means to be a "good woman."

Then on this path of internalizing harm—which we imagine will secure for us lasting love—we work so hard to erase ourselves, to stuff down our desires and feelings, to muffle our voices and our dreams, and to even sacrifice parts of our very own souls, thus giving up our spiritual wellness. All of this we do in hopes of becoming more "feminine" and less ourselves.

Seeking Male Approval Can Become Self-Destructive and Addictive

"Every time I prayed *Istikhaarah* about whether or not to marry my husband," my friend said, "I felt a stronger dislike toward the idea."

Then my friend (whom I'll call Afifa) said something to me that I don't think I'll ever forget: "That's how I knew I should marry my husband. Because if I didn't and I instead chose a man I was really attracted to, I would be following my desires."

Till today, Afifa's words break my heart, because I know all too well where this thinking comes from. In performing femininity, the obligation of all Muslims (male and female) to stay away from feeding *sinful* desires is often conflated with a righteous woman's obligation to stay away from *any* desires that contradict a man's, especially if that man is (or desires to be) her husband.

Desire for Male Approval Is Stronger Than Her Desire

When a woman is performing femininity, the desire for external male approval often becomes so strong that she will consciously and *eagerly* suppress her own needs and desires in the process. She will also deliberately abandon and deny parts of her true self if she knows (or imagines) that her authenticity would displease men.

Over time, the woman becomes so adept at disowning the deepest parts of herself that self-abandonment becomes a seamless effort that she eventually does unconsciously. At this stage, her self-erasure becomes an emotional addiction that essentially tells her mind and nervous system that "less is more." In other words, the less she seeks what she actually wants or needs for own life and wellbeing, the more of a "real woman" she is.

For the Muslim woman, this addiction is made all the more problematic when she also mentally processes her self-erasure as pious sacrifice "for the sake of Allah." In this mental state, the more pangs of discomfort she feels as a result of her choices, the more her discomfort serves as proof of her own spiritual goodness as a "righteous woman." However, over time, she is unable to maintain this level of self-erasure, so she becomes overwhelmed by emotional exhaustion. Additionally, her spiritual life often begins to suffer as she becomes enveloped by feelings of spiritual emptiness, confusion, and/or frustration.

For many women, this is also the stage where both their mental and physical health begin to suffer in ways that can no longer be ignored or trivialized. Yet nearly all of this unwellness came about as a result of the woman overextending herself on the path of "righteous martyrdom" as a good wife and mother. Consequently, she becomes like the people who are so generous and giving to others that they put their own selves in extreme hardship and harm's way as a result. Not surprisingly, in the Qur'an, Allah Himself warns the human being (male and female) against this type of personal extremism:

$$\text{وَلَا تَجْعَلْ يَدَكَ مَغْلُولَةً إِلَىٰ عُنُقِكَ وَلَا تَبْسُطْهَا كُلَّ ٱلْبَسْطِ فَتَقْعُدَ مَلُومًا مَّحْسُورًا ﴿٢٩﴾}$$

"And do not make your hand [as] chained to your neck or extend it completely to its utmost reach and

[thereby] become blameworthy and insolvent (or destitute)."
—Al-Israa (17:29)

Yet, for the woman whose entire identity and self-worth are rooted in overextending herself in the path of making other people's lives easier, not even the risk of her own emotional unwellness or spiritual destitution can deter her. In fact, for women whose womanhood is linked to performing femininity, pleasing men will almost always be a higher priority than being emotional well and spiritually nourished herself. Most seriously, for the Muslim woman living in this state, pleasing men becomes a higher priority than pleasing Allah.

This is why, for example, it is commonplace for "good women" to give up their rights, lower their standards, and trivialize divine mercies (e.g., a woman having her own wealth) in an effort to increase their chances of getting (and staying) married. This is because it is well-known in circles of performing femininity amongst Muslim women that the most highly praised woman is the one who looks at the rights that Allah grants her and at the divine mercies He offers her, yet she figuratively waves a hand of dismissal at it all while fixating on only one question, "What will please the man I want to marry?" And if it pleases that man for her to dismiss most (or all) of what Allah offers her, then that's what she will do—even if deep inside she wants something more for herself and her life.

In this mental space, the promises of a man are more meaningful and valuable to the woman's heart than the promises of Allah. Yet in her anxious pursuit of enjoying the promises of a man, she convinces herself that all of her sacrifice (i.e., self-erasure) is proof that she has full faith in the promises of Allah. However, the reality is that, deep down, she is unwilling to sit patiently in the discomfort of faithfully trusting in the promise of Allah—because this would mean sitting patiently in the discomfort of displeasing or upsetting a man (or the collective male gaze). Even if all of her deepest desires for her life and marriage are *halaal* and potentially pleasing to Allah, she will give up every single one of them if she imagines that her pursuit of any of them *might* displease a man.

In other words, to the woman who knows (or accepts) no definition of womanhood or piety other than righteous martyrdom and performing femininity, the social and personal benefits of self-erasure are simply too great to give up, even in the face of promises of worldly goodness and blessed provision from Allah. So, even though her Creator Himself promises multiple rewards in this life and in the Hereafter to people of faith endowed with both patience and *tawakkul* (sincere trust in Him), neither of these qualities is prioritized in a woman performing femininity while pursuing marriage. She allows herself to consciously embrace these two qualities only *after* she is trapped in an unhealthy relationship, an unfortunate circumstance that she likely would not have experienced if she had embraced patience and tawakkul *before* she entered the relationship in the first place (or at all).

Tragically, in her "pious" life path of righteous martyrdom and performing femininity, the seeds of spiritual crisis were planted. As a result, it is highly likely that one day this same woman will imagine that Islam is to blame for her painful life circumstances. Yet it was Islam itself that she trivialized when she first chose it.

Read more at uzauthor.com

About the Author

Known for her soul-touching books and spiritual reflections on emotional healing, Umm Zakiyyah is a world-renowned author, speaker, and soul-care mentor. She specializes in supporting women of faith transform into the best version of themselves—personally, emotionally, and spiritually.

Also known by her birth name Ruby Moore and her "Muslim name" Baiyinah Siddeeq, Umm Zakiyyah is the internationally acclaimed, award-winning author of more than forty books, including novels, short stories, and self-help. Her books are used in high schools and universities in the United States and worldwide, and her work has been translated into multiple languages.

Her novel *His Other Wife* is now a short film (available on Prime Video).

Umm Zakiyyah is certified in Rapid Transformational Therapy ® (RTT) and hypnotherapy, qualifications she earned under the guidance of Marisa Peer, author of *I Am Enough*. She also holds a certificate in trauma and somatics.

Umm Zakiyyah studied Arabic, Qur'an, Islamic sciences, *'aqeedah,* and *tafseer* in the USA, Egypt, and Saudi Arabia for more than fifteen years.

Umm Zakiyyah has a BA degree in Elementary Education, an MA in English Language Learning, and Cambridge's CELTA (Certificate in English Language Teaching to Adults).

She is currently based in Dallas, Texas (USA).

Connect with Umm Zakiyyah online:
UZ books: uzauthor.com
Feminine Soul Reset: sqsoul.com
Instagram: @uzauthor
TikTok: @uzauthor

Glossary of Arabic and Islamic Terms

alhamdulillah: "All praise belongs to Allah (God, the Creator) alone"

Allah: Arabic term for God; the only One who has the right to be worshipped; the Creator of the universe and all in existence

amaanah: a divine trust and responsibility

'aqeedah: foundational beliefs or creed

ayah/ayaat: verse(s) from Qur'an or divine sign(s)

bid'ah: sinful innovation in religion

baseerah: insight or clarity of vision

da'wah: teaching others about Islam; inviting others to spiritual guidance

deen: spiritual way of life; religion

dhulm: wrongdoing or oppression (of others or one's own soul)

'ebaadah: worship or sincere obedience to Allah

emaan: sincere faith; authentic spirituality; belief in Islam; *Tawheed*

ghuroor: spiritual self-deception

halaal: divinely blessed or permissible

haraam: divinely forbidden or sinful

hasad: envy that is sinful and spiritually destructive

ijmaa': unanimous agreement amongst the earliest Muslims and scholars; scholarly consensus

ikhlaas: spiritual sincerity

inshaa'Allah: God-willing

kibr: sinful pride or pride that is spiritually harmful; looking down on others and rejecting the truth

nafs: human inner self made up of the complex interconnectedness of a person's soul, mind, heart, and body; sometimes refers to a person's desires that are self-serving and spiritually harmful

qadar: divine decree; predestination

qawwaam/qawwaamah: the man's divinely assigned role of being the maintainer, provider, and protector of women in the home and society

Qiyaam ul-Layl: the blessed night prayer, prayed in last third of night

Rabb: another name for Allah that refers to His Lordship over creation; Creator, Owner and Manager of all that exists

riyaa: insincerity; showing off; seeking the pleasure, admiration, reward, or attention of other than Allah

salaf: earliest generations of Muslims

shirk: assigning divine attributes to creation or creation's attributes to the Creator; paganism

soo'u dhann: assuming the worst about someone or something or assigning the worst possible meaning or intention to someone or something

SubhaanAllah: statement of glorification of Allah: "Glory to Allah, and Exalted and High is He above any imperfection"

sujood: another term for *sajdah:* prostrating the forehead on the floor in submission to Allah

Sunnah: prophetic guidance or example; the life and teachings of Prophet Muhammad (peace and blessings be upon him)

taqwaa: sincere God-consciousness and daily soul care that protects the heart from corruption and the soul from spiritual harm in the Hereafter

tawakkul: sincere trust in the wisdom and decisions of the Creator

Tawheed: Oneness of Allah; singling out the Creator alone in worship; authentic monotheism; sincere belief in the Oneness of Allah

ummah: all Muslims from every generation; worldwide faith community

REFERENCES

Al-Awadi, H. (2007). *Women Inspired By the Beloved.*

Ibn al-Qayyim (1930). *Rawdat al-Muhibeen*

Stats on Suicide in Men (2023). HeadsUpGuys. The University
of British Columbia. Retrieved July 31, 2023 from
https://headsupguys.org/suicide-stats-men/

www.ingramcontent.com/pod-product-compliance
Lightning Source LLC
Chambersburg PA
CBHW032054090426
42744CB00005B/213